CW00530184

Claire Lilley's comprehensive career has spanned over thirty years. During that time she has been involved in many aspects of equestrianism, from competitive jumping and dressage to running livery yards and riding stables. She now runs her own training yard in Wiltshire offering training for young horses, remedial training and rider training on her own schoolmasters. She competes on all her horses at various levels up to Grand Prix in dressage and in dressage to music. Claire believes in developing a good understanding and relationship between horse and rider and, based on this principle, has developed a range of training products, instructional DVDs and her new CD, *Riding to Music*. Claire is the author of the best-selling book *Schooling with Ground Poles* and *The Problem-free Horse*, also published by J.A. Allen. Claire is a listed dressage judge and runs regular clinics in Sweden. To find out more about Claire, visit her website: www.clairelilley.com.

CLAIRE LILLEY

DRESSAGE to MUSIC

*Build a Freestyle from
Choreography to Competition*

J.A. Allen

© *Claire Lilley, 2008*

First published in Great Britain 2008

ISBN 978-0-85131-943-8

J.A. Allen
Clerkenwell House
Clerkenwell Green
London EC1R 0HT

www.halebooks.com

J.A. Allen is an imprint of Robert Hale Limited

A catalogue record for this book is available from the British Library

Design by Judy Linard
Photographs by, or property of, the author, except for those on page 36 (Lena Hulterstrom),
page 63 (DE Photos), page 97 (publisher), pages 99 and 101 (Sylvia Loch), on pages 108, 122
and 155 (John Parker), page 153 (lower) (Forge Digital), page 156 (BRC), page 159 (Julia Rau),
page 160 (Kit Houghton), page 163 (Elizabeth Furth) and page 165 (Arthur Kottas)
Line illustrations by Rachael Tremlett
Edited by Martin Diggle
Printed by New Era Printing Co. Limited, Hong Kong

CONTENTS

ACKNOWLEDGEMENTS

This book has been a joy to write, but has needed quite a bit of research along the way, so I do thank everyone whose brains I have picked en route.

I am very grateful to Arthur Kottas, for his help with the book and for training me for quite a few years now; to Jennie Loriston-Clarke for her instruction and assistance with my test riding, and for her insight into riding at international level; to Richard Davison for his helpful comments, trade secrets and answers to my numerous questions; and to Ingrid Klimke for her kind words and perceptions of top-level competition. I would also like to thank Sylvia Loch, one of my mentors, who gave me the confidence and opportunity to ride in public. An authority on Portuguese equitation, Sylvia also kindly checked the text relating to the Portuguese School of Equestrian Art, and supplied the photos relating to that School and the Royal Andalusian School. Thanks also to my friend and former team mate, Bridget Parry-James, for her imput into Chapter 8.

My thanks go to Martin Diggle for his witty remarks that make going through the editing process a pleasurable experience, and Cassandra Campbell of J. A. Allen who has encouraged me throughout the writing of this book.

Thanks for allowing me to use their photos go to John Parker for the photos of the Chipstead Riding Club Quadrille team, Forge Digital for the 'Mary Poppins' shots, DE Photos for the 'Egyptian' shot and my husband, Dougald Ballardie, for the majority of the photos and also the cover shots.

I'd also like to thank Jason Bell, my local computer expert, who came to the rescue when my computer crashed comprehensively midway through writing!

Finally, I am grateful to all the horses and riders who attend my clinic at Nobynäs Stud in Sweden, who are always ready and willing to perform a Quadrille at the drop of a hat. In fact, thank you to all the riders, instructors and helpers I have known and ridden with for their help over the years, and their contribution to the enjoyment of riding to music – and thanks, of course, to the horses. I hope they have had as much fun as I have.

INTRODUCTION

*D*ressage to music is continually growing in popularity, and is very appealing to spectators. The first international Freestyle dressage to music competition, known as the 'Kür' was at Goodwood CDI in 1979. Nowadays, the Kür is the deciding factor in the individual medals at the World and European Championships, and at the Olympic Games.

Dressage to music competitions are great fun for spectators and competitors alike, and appeal to a wide audience. You do not have to understand the intricacies of dressage to enjoy watching horses and riders performing to music. Nevertheless, many people are put off riding to music because it seems too complicated. The task of putting together a set routine appears daunting, as does selecting suitable music. However, using music has other applications, apart from just competing. Schooling to music adds another dimension to daily training, and helps both horse and rider to remain calm and develop a sense of rhythm and fluency in their work. Riding to different tracks for fun helps the rider choose which style of music suits their horse – though more often than not it is the horse who shows his own preference.

Some horses are more musical than others, in the same way that people are. A 'musical' horse picks up the beat of any track, and alters his stride to suit. A non-musical horse needs the help of the rider to give him the rhythm with well-timed aids. (Any readers who think this rather fanciful may be interested to learn that the early Renaissance trainer, Césare Fiaschi, introduced music to his lessons specifically to promote rhythm, and other classical trainers have acknowledged the role of music in training.)

This book aims to encourage everyone to have a go to riding to music (even if just for fun and to add another dimension to everyday schooling), to remove the mystery behind creating a routine for competition and to give a comprehensive, easy-to-follow guide to entering your first competition. Included are first-hand experiences from well-known riders and trainers, as well as the experiences of everyday riders who have competed for the first time. The book describes how to ride to music in a group, explains Quadrille riding, gives advice on designing and making costumes that do not cost the earth and explains the rules, choreography and the technical side of producing the music to ride to.

Music adds another dimension to schooling your horse at home so, if you find yourself wondering what to work on next, just put some music on and give it a go!

1

SCHOOLING TO MUSIC

RIDING TO MUSIC when you school helps tremendously with many aspects of training your horse. First of all, it accustoms him to music coming from your playing system and is therefore useful 'anti-spook' training for when you go to a competition with a public address system. I have seen many horses who perform very well at home, but 'freak out' when faced with loudspeakers booming at them in a show ring. Whether you show horses, showjump, ride cross-country, or do dressage, you will always come across public address systems, so music can help whatever discipline you like to do. It can help you to develop a sense of rhythm, and to maintain regularity in your horse's steps when riding different school movements. It can help accuracy, for example counting the number of beats it takes to make a 10 m circle helps you to ride each one the same size. It can even be beneficial in jumping training, helping you to keep a regular stride into a jump.

How to Begin

You will need a CD player/iPod dock (or, for those of us still using them, a cassette player) positioned in the schooling area, somewhere it can be heard easily. I place mine on top of a large barrel in the corner of the school, so I can reach the control buttons from my horse. This eliminates the need to keep hopping on and off every time I want to change track. A good supply of batteries is also necessary if you do not have access to an electrical power supply. There is nothing worse than being in mid-hum to your favourite track when it starts to slur into something resembling Barry White singing in a coal mine.

Another option is to use a Walkman or iPod with headphones, which is a quick, convenient way of listening to the music, though I find it useful for my horse to hear the music as well. It is much more beneficial from a training point of view for both you and your horse to hear the music. If you have a horse who picks up the beat of the music easily, this can help you to improve your own sense of rhythm. If your horse is not so musically inclined, he will improve if you can help him by riding well.

To save riding for hours to every track on an album, spend some time at home selecting a variety of tracks that you may like to try, such as a mixture of pop, jazz and classical, or theme tunes from TV programmes, films or commercials. Select some with vocals and some instrumental tracks. A regular beat helps you to relax and 'trust the music' as you are not waiting for any tricky bits to occur. Try to avoid music where the rhythm changes all of a sudden for a few seconds. This can throw you and put you at a loss as to what to ride to it that fits. An example of this is 'Bohemian Rhapsody' by Queen. Much as I love this track to listen to, I find it tricky to ride to. However, if the music you select has fast and slow sections, but with a regular beat, it can be a useful exercise to adapt your ridden work to match the music, i.e. riding the trot a bit quicker or slower by using variations within the gait. For example, tracks that have a mixture of quiet and loud sections can inspire you to ride extension and collection. Kylie Minogue's record, 'Can't Get You Out Of My Head' has a super regular beat throughout, and is a great track to use to get you into the swing of riding to music. Big band music, such as Glen Miller's, is used a lot in competition, for the same reason. You could create a playlist on your iPod or burn these onto a CD. I have actually produced my own CD, *Riding to Music*, which is 45 minutes long (sufficient for a schooling session with your horse) and has tracks specially composed for training purposes, with suggestions as to what to ride to each track, as well as a couple of routines to try. This is available for purchase from my website, www.clairelilley.com.

Calm, relaxing music can sooth a fizzy horse and improve relaxation. Also, if you feel in need of a bit of TLC, music can be as therapeutic for the rider. On the other hand, disco music with a strong, punchy beat helps to develop impulsion, and can make a lazy horse work with more energy as well as inspiring the rider to ride more positively. Some tracks you will find seem to fit any gait, so just play around with walk, trot and canter.

Try to distinguish between each phrase of the music. A phrase is where part of a tune or song has a consistent melody and tone. It then changes to maybe a slower phrase, or a quieter one, before becoming louder and punchier again. This type of track is great for transition work, either from one gait to another, or within a gait, for example working trot to medium trot and back again. Riding changes of stride within each gait, such as collected, working, medium and extended trot to the same track can help the steps to remain regular.

The following exercises can be ridden in either a short (20x40 m) or long (20x60 m) arena.

Keeping the energy in shoulder-in is much easier when riding to an upbeat piece of music, as shown here with Heinrich.

Work in Walk

So now you are in your school with your horse, armed with CD player or iPod deck and music to experiment with. If your horse has never seen a CD player before, let him sniff it, but be careful he does not knock it over, or accidentally hit the 'play' button, which may scare him. Have the volume on low, and turn the music on, so he becomes accustomed to the sound. Once he is relaxed, turn it up gradually, then mount up and ride around the school in walk, passing the CD player without tensing up yourself. If you are anxious, your horse will pick this up, so it is important that you are both relaxed from the beginning. With a spooky horse, I have found from personal experience that having music to listen to helps the horse to relax and concentrate on his work rather than looking for things to be afraid of. The music also helps the rider to relax and to ride with a better sense of rhythm.

While you are walking around the school, be aware of your horse's walk steps, and see if it is easy to keep in time with the music. Practise walking straight lines and large circles, keeping in rhythm as best you can. You may find this difficult at first, but if you think of moving your hips with the beat this can help. Most horses will pick up the rhythm themselves provided that you do not interfere too much, but you have to move your back with the horse's movement otherwise you will restrict his steps and shorten his length of stride, especially if you become tense. Walk the same exercises on the other rein. This is a good way of checking whether either you or your horse is less supple in one direction or the other. This becomes more obvious the smaller the circles you ride.

EXERCISES TO TRY IN WALK

1. Starting at X, walk a 20 m circle on each rein, changing direction on returning to X. Then reduce the diameter of the circles to 15 m in each direction, and then to 10 m. Try to keep the same length of stride and rhythm as the circles become smaller.

2. Walk a square in each direction, changing through X again; trying to keep the rhythm through the corners; this is more difficult as most horses shorten their steps on a small turn. The squares can either be ridden as two half-school figures with rounded corners or true squares, which involve quarter-turns on the haunches at the corners. You can collect the steps on the corners, but keep the same rhythm. Collection does not mean taking small, pottery steps – collection means the horse takes more weight on his hind legs and lifts through his forehand, making shorter, higher steps, so these steps should be in the same rhythm as medium walk. Ride medium walk on the straight sides of the square.

3. Walk up the long side, and before the corner, ride a 10 m half-circle, before returning to the track. Ride this in each direction, trying to take the same number of steps for each half-circle. You could return to the track in half-pass to make the exercise more difficult, or instead of 10 m half-circles ride a walk half-pirouette each time.

4. Walk shoulder-in up the long side, then ride a 10 m circle, followed by travers. This really does test the quality of your lateral work, as it is so easy to lose forwardness when going sideways!

Four exercises to try in walk.

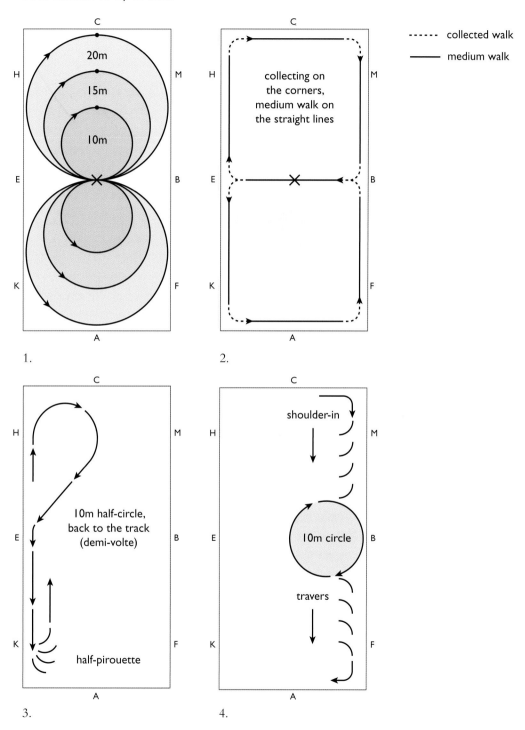

----- collected walk

——— medium walk

1.

2. collecting on
the corners,
medium walk on
the straight lines

3. 10m half-circle,
back to the track
(demi-volte)

half-pirouette

4. shoulder-in

10m circle

travers

Follow the exercises with walking on a long rein, which is useful to allow your horse to stretch through his back and neck and to develop extended walk steps, which I think of as a free walk into the bridle, keeping the horse taking big steps that over-track with his neck reaching forwards to the bit, and not becoming short and tight. Music can be a huge training aid in helping you to keep the walk rhythm as you do this.

Trot Work

If the music does not suit your horse's walk, proceed into trot and see if this fits any better. A mistake a lot of people make is to go too fast as soon as they go into trot, and not listen to the beat, so try to let your horse do his natural trot at first without interfering too much and see if he adjusts his steps to match the rhythm. Work in either rising or sitting trot, as you prefer, and move in time to the music. If you have difficulty yourself in getting the timing right, it may help to boogie around the living room at home to improve your own sense of rhythm!

EXERCISES TO TRY IN TROT

Many pieces of music suit trot work. You may find some a bit quick or rather slow, but practise altering the trot to fit the music sometimes. Do this within reason – you do not want to be dashing around with your horse's legs going like a sewing machine, nor do you want him barely trotting but, as a rule, slower trot music fits well with passage, piaffe or extended trot. (These movements require more power from the horse, so it is necessary to slow the steps to obtain sufficient engagement – in particular, extension is not achieved by allowing/encouraging the horse to 'run off'.) Trot work can be vastly improved by counting the beats as you school. For example, ride a 10 m circle and count how many steps it takes you to do. Then ride another one in the other direction. This is how to make sure your circles are all consistent in size, and of correct shape. Use the music to help you stay in rhythm, so the strides are all the same size. Riding collected, medium, and extended trot to the same piece of music is a real test of balance – if your horse falls on his forehand when you ask for medium trot, he will speed up and get ahead of the beat. If he loses impulsion in collected trot, he will go too slowly.

1. In a 40x20 m arena, ride a three-loop serpentine in trot, keeping the

same rhythm on the straight parts as on the curves. This sounds easier that it is. If you are in a long (60x20 m) arena, ride four or five loops. Another option is to add circles inside the loops.

2. Ride several changes of rein using the short diagonals of the school, ending up with a diamond pattern. Try to maintain the same power and rhythm through the corners, even though you will be collecting a bit on the corners for balance. Ride working trot on the straight parts. Then you could ride medium or extended steps across the short diagonals, collecting again for the corners, which is a good test of control. You could finish the exercise with a long diagonal in medium or extended trot, especially if you have a good, rousing piece of music!

3. Ride shoulder-in up the long side one third of the way, then change the rein across the school and ride the last third of the next long side in shoulder-out – the idea being that you have maintained the bend of the horse throughout the exercise, and hopefully the rhythm and balance in time with the music! Change bend as you come to the short side, and repeat on the other rein.

Four exercises to try in trot.

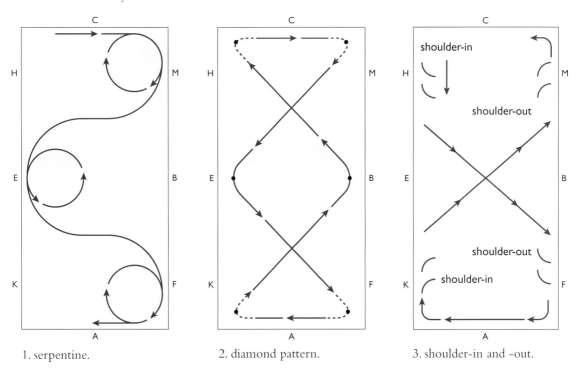

1. serpentine.　　2. diamond pattern.　　3. shoulder-in and -out.

——— working trot　　------ collected trot

Continued.

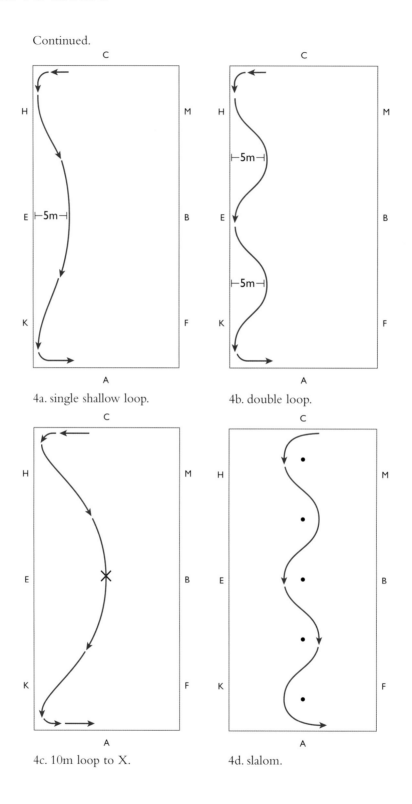

4a. single shallow loop.

4b. double loop.

4c. 10m loop to X.

4d. slalom.

4.   Ride a shallow loop 5 m in from the track at its widest point at E or B, halfway along the side, without changing rhythm. Then you could try double loops of 5 m on the long sides. Then ride a 10 m loop to X. Do these on both reins. Then try a slalom up the centre line, i.e. a series of loops. You may like to place a line of markers up the centre line to weave in and out of. A more advanced exercise is to leg-yield in from the track, and back out, or half-pass in and out. (Or leg-yield in, half-pass out – there are several variations you can try.) Make sure that you ride corners and changes of direction with precision. Take time to ride accurately. This takes up more music, but there is no point in cutting corners just to keep up with the track that is playing. This is the beauty of letting the music just continue while you are riding – you are not up against a set time limit, so you have a chance to really get the feel of the movements.

Canter Work

The rhythms of walk and canter are similar, i.e. the beat of the walk is 1, 2, 3, 4 and that of the canter is 1, 2, 3, up (try riding canter to a three-beat waltz and four-beat quickstep and see which is easier), so you should find you can canter easily to the music you walked to. This is very useful when riding walk-canter-walk transitions. Cantering continually for 5 minutes to a whole track will feel a very long time at first, and be quite physically demanding for you and your horse if you only do short spells of canter when you school. Using music is a good way to increase your staying power and your horse's fitness, but build up gradually, and be aware of your horse getting out of breath, so do stop and take a break regularly. As with trot work, there is no need to set off at a gallop as soon as the music starts! It is a common fault to try to canter too fast in general schooling, so cantering to music is a good way of slowing the tempo of your canter, and teaching your horse to remain in better balance, taking weight more on his hind legs. If he is on his forehand you will find it impossible to change within the canter gait, e.g. from working canter to collected canter. It can be a useful exercise

Heinrich and me having fun in canter.

21

to try to collect for just a few steps at first, then resume working canter.

There is usually a huge improvement to the canter rhythm when riding to music, whether you ride basic exercises, or more advanced ones such as canter pirouettes or flying changes. Music often gives the canter more 'lift' and lightness, which are essentials for more advanced work. Music is of great benefit to sequences of flying changes where it is imperative to keep the rhythm spot on. The music must be easy to canter to, though, so that your horse remains relaxed and can change easily. If the music is too fast he may become tense and not change cleanly. If it is too slow, he may cope, but you could lose energy.

EXERCISES TO TRY IN CANTER

1. Ride a 20 m circle in canter at one end of the school, noting how many steps you take on each half of the circle. It is all too easy to ride the first half too big, and the second half too small. Marking out a 20 m circle with ground poles (see diagram) is useful in this case, as you can check how many steps you need for each quarter of the circle. Then proceed to the other end of the school and ride a 15 m circle on the same rein, and feel how much music that takes up. It should be less than the 20 m circle! Then return to the poles and ride a 10 m circle around one of them. The pole can help you to ride both sides of the circle the same, as before, but see how much less music you need. Change the rein and repeat.

2. Ride a 10 m circle in each corner of the school, and one halfway up the long side. This is a good test to see if your circles fit the music. You should find a 10 m circle takes about six to eight strides, or six to eight beats of the music. Once you have worked out which fits the best, try to get each circle the same.

3. Try riding a 'square' serpentine, by turning across the school. Change legs through walk or trot over the centre line. As mentioned before, walk and canter should fit to the same music, so these two gaits should work well together. (A more advanced exercise is to ride a flying change each time.)

4. Ride a 10 m circle at the beginning of the long side, and go into a 5 m shallow loop. Finish the loop with another circle at the end of the long side. Another version is to start with a 10 m circle, ride a 10 m loop to X, circle again, then return to the track, This could be ridden as a half-pass in from the track, 10 m circle at X, and half-pass back.

Four exercises to try in canter.

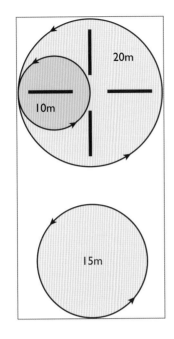

1.

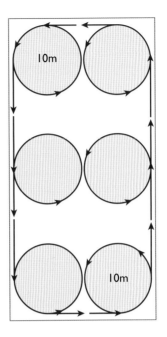

2.

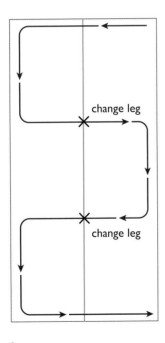

3.

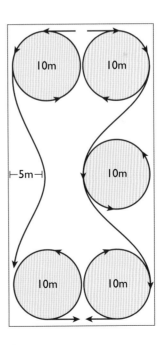

4.

—— working canter

Jumping to Music

When I was in the Pony Club we used to compete regularly in Prix Caprilli competitions, which consisted of a dressage-type test with a couple of small jumps or cavalletti over which you had to trot or canter according to the particular test you were riding. I think this is such a good way of training horses and riders to jump accurately, that I have included it in this book, with the addition of music!

It is very important to approach a jump in rhythm and balance, whether out of trot or canter, so music is an ideal way to keep the rider calm, and to prevent over-riding at fences, especially if you have a track of music with a clear, punchy beat.

JUMPING EXERCISES TO TRY

Build a small jump halfway up each long side of the school. This can be either on the track so that the school wall acts as a wing to prevent your horse dodging out, or you could leave a gap so the track is free to ride along. The height of the jumps is totally up to you. A good technique is often better developed over small jumps (no more than 0.5 m [1 ft 8 in]) rather than trying to be too ambitious and losing confidence. The jumps should be small uprights or parallels, or one of each that can be jumped from either direction.

1. In canter to the music, ride a circle at one end of the school then proceed to the first jump without speeding up or slowing down. After the jump, continue in the same rhythm, and ride another circle at the other end of the school. The size of the circles can be 10, 12, or 15 m in diameter, but try to make them both the same size, so they take up the same amount of music. Repeat on the other rein.

2. Using the same jump layout, canter a circle (any size) at one end of the school, and then proceed over the first jump. Ride a 10 m half-circle, then canter back over the jump. Change leg through trot, walk or with a flying change. Proceed to the second jump and repeat. You can develop this exercise to include half-pass towards the jump after the 10 m half-circle, or ride a large canter pirouette instead of the half-circle.

3. Set four small jumps or cavalletti in a box formation in the centre of the school so you have two small doubles that can be approached in

either direction, each with one non–jumping stride in between. The music will really help you to jump both combinations in a good rhythm, with the same stride in between. The music can help to prevent speeding up or slowing down.

4. Set three small jumps side on down the centre line. Ride a serpentine over the jumps, changing legs over each jump, or at least before the next one! Again, this can be through trot, walk or a flying change. Use the music to help you to keep your turns accurate, and try not to allow your horse to fall in. It helps if you remember not to lean in, of course! It can be useful to ride a small circle of 10 to 12 m in between the jumps if you overshoot your line of approach.

2

SELECTING MUSIC FOR COMPETITIONS

*H*opefully, you have now been schooling your horse to music (see previous chapter) on a regular basis to get the feel of what you like to ride to, and how to pick up the beat of the music. Your horse may react adversely to some tracks, and enjoy others, and the only way to find out is to try. For competitive riding, you need to find music that allows your horse to work comfortably in walk, trot and canter, so that it is easy to ride different movements without worrying about making too many adjustments to his gaits. It is all too easy to ride at a different speed at a competition because of nerves, not listening to the music properly and losing the beat. If you are unsure what a medium walk, working trot, working canter, etc. should look like, it may be worth going along to a dressage competition and watching a few competitors to get an idea of what you are aiming at in the three gaits. Also, have a look at the collected and extended steps in each gait. Common mistakes are to go too fast in medium or extended trot and canter, and to dawdle along in a free walk on a long rein. A lot of riders fail to keep the same rhythm when riding different movements, such as circles, so this is something to bear in mind with your own riding technique.

Work on the Lunge

A good way to find out if the music fits your horse's gaits is to lunge him to it. This has the added advantage of you being on the ground and thus able to change your music easily. After loosening him up with no auxiliary reins, either use side reins, or double lunge (my book *The Problem-Free Horse* explains lungeing techniques in detail) so that he is working in a correct outline as he would when you are in the saddle. Lungeing to the music can give you a clearer idea of your horse's natural rhythm than actually riding him, as it is all too easy to alter the horse's rhythm unintentionally when in the saddle. For example, if you are feeling a bit jaded, you may ride slower and with less impulsion than usual. If you are tense, you may ride faster. If you are not paying attention to his way of going you may allow your horse's steps either to shorten or become long and flat.

Play a piece of music that you like, and allow your horse to walk to it. While you are lungeing him, watch his footsteps, particularly his hind feet, and see if they step in time with the music. Just keep him going in a medium walk, which should be his normal walk. If the music does not fit with his steps, try other tracks until you find one that does. However, if your horse's normal walk is at a snail's pace you will have to gee him up a bit. If he is tense and walking too fast, then use half-halts on the lunge line to steady him and help him to find a better rhythm.

Particularly if his walk is not naturally long-striding and athletic and he finds it difficult to walk to the music you are playing, you may find that your horse offers canter instead. The timing of the steps in walk and canter are very similar, so you may find that he can walk to what you think is canter music and vice versa. Once you have found a

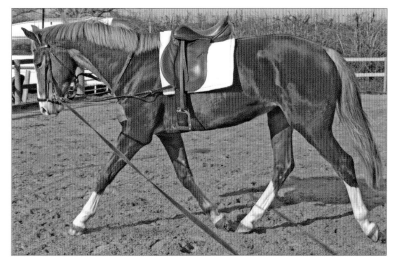

Lungeing to the music can give you a clear idea of your horse's natural rhythm. Spartan Archer (Archie) enjoying the musical accompaniment.

27

suitable piece of music for walking to, try asking your horse to extend and collect his walk steps, and see if he can maintain the same rhythm. Watch for his inside hind leg stepping onto the ground in time with the music every fourth beat. Count this as beat one, then the inside foreleg on beat two, outside hind on beat three, and outside foreleg on beat four.

It makes sense to select music for canter next: a track that may be too rousing for walk may suit canter very well. Although (as explained in the previous chapter) the *timing* of the canter and walk are similar, the *mood* of the music may vary, so choosing calmer passages for walk and more upbeat ones for canter may work well. Also, listen for quiet and louder bits that can be used for collection and extension respectively, but choose a regular beat that fits your horse's normal working canter. In fitting the canter's three beats plus a moment of suspension to four-beat music, a lot of people watch for the inside foreleg stepping forwards on beat one, but this can give the impression of your horse being heavier on his forehand. Instead, try watching his inside hind leg stepping onto the ground on beat one – this gives the impression of more power coming from the hindquarters. Watch both and compare the difference in visual impression!

Some slow waltz music can also be suitable for certain exercises – the 'Blue Danube' by Strauss, for example. Although it is three-beat, it has a lilting quality which lends itself well to the suspension in the canter required for flying changes. This music is one of my favourites to ride to as a complete piece (as opposed to chopping bits out of it to make up a routine for competition), and I have used it in demonstrations, as it has phrases that you can walk, trot and canter to, as well as highs and lows.

Many tracks are suitable for trot. Again, when choosing trot music, select a track that your horse finds it easy to trot to, using energetic phrases to ask for medium or extended strides, and lighter phrases for collection. Slow trot music often suits passage and piaffe, where you have more suspension. Watch the hind legs of your horse rather than the forelegs, and you will get a better idea as he is stepping with more weight on his hind legs. If you watch the forelegs, they can look flashy, but he may not be working properly from behind, which is what the judge will be looking for.

Heinrich in working trot.

Heinrich in collected trot.

Heinrich in medium trot, on the lunge.

USING FILM

Another way to choose your music is to ask a willing friend to film your horse while you either lunge or ride him to show his natural gaits, in walk, trot and canter. You can then watch the film at home, music system to hand, and play different tracks until you find music that matches his gaits.

Riding to the Music

Once you have a few suitable tracks, put them all onto one music system, and ride to them. To help you make your final selection, put two or three possible choices for each gait onto your system so it is easy to ride to them without having to get off and fiddle around with your machine. It now comes down to personal preference and which type of music fits with your horse's character and outlook on life! Do not worry too much about different movements at this stage – the aim is to select the music. For example, I used to ride a pretty Welsh pony called Monty, whose dainty footwork fitted very well with Strauss's 'Pizzicato Polka'. Our Dutch Warmblood, Trevor, on the other hand, is partial to a bit of Western music, and thunders along happily to 'The Big Country'. Part Lipizzaner Amadeus manages to fit to anything, usually resorting to passage when nothing else will do, and Trakehner Heinrich is a bit of a smoothie, and swanks along to theme tunes from James Bond films. I used to have a Lusitano, Leo, who loved classical music but became very tense and unreasonable if I played either Michael Jackson or Queen. You may personally prefer classical music, or jazz for example. The main thing is to have fun and enjoy yourself – you will ride much better if you actually like the music.

You can use music to enhance your horse's strongest gait, and also to disguise his weakest. If your music has loud and quiet bits in it, you could use the loud music to give the impression of power in extended walk, and quiet music to emphasize lightness in collection. If your horse has a poor rhythm in walk, it can be useful to choose music with a punchy beat so that you can help him improve his steps. Amadeus walks much better to something with a good beat – he tends to wander along aimlessly otherwise! Using 'background' music or something too airy-fairy can make the walk look more uneven than it actually is. However, if your horse has a very strong, powerful canter, for example, you could use background music, which would not detract from the canter steps, as they have enough strength to give a good impression on their own. Strong music with a strong canter can be a bit over the top, especially if your horse's walk and trot are not of the same calibre. It is all very well enhancing the good bits, but you do not want to be too extreme and make the other gaits appear flat and boring.

If your horse has a quick 'sewing machine' type of trot, fast music will just make it look very hectic, so choose something just a bit slower, and try to keep yourself in the rhythm. (This, as mentioned in the previous chapter, is how music can help to improve your horse's way of going.) If, on the other hand, your horse's trot is heavy and laboured, invigorating music will help to give the appearance of energy.

Music can enhance your horse's good points, and disguise the weaker points to an extent, but if you have a real problem with his way of going, then correct school-ing is the only way to improve things!

Selecting tracks from similar types of music helps the finished routine appear more professional. For example 'Zorba the Greek', mixed with a classical piece, followed by Western music does not really blend well! If you can find three tracks on the same CD that suit walk, trot and canter, not only will they blend well together but the sound levels will be the same, i.e. you will not end up with a quiet walk that no one can hear and an extremely loud canter. The person in charge of playing the music at a competition is not going to be able to turn the sound up and down accordingly during your test, as they will not be familiar with your routine! They usually set the volume at an appropriate level for the beginning of the test, and then let it play. (This question of volume can be altered technically though – the technicalities of creating music are discussed in Chapter 4).

For competition, instrumental tracks are preferred, but vocals that blend well with the music, such as 'doo-bee-do-ing,' are perfectly all right to use. In unaffiliated competitions, the rules are more relaxed about allowing vocals, so you have more freedom to choose whatever you like to ride to, to encourage you to have a go. Some tunes sound strange without vocals – for example, I have used our Quadrille music, *Mary Poppins*, which has vocals all the way through, in conventional affiliated competition at Prix St Georges level and scored well for choice of music, so I do think it is a matter of whether or not vocals suits the performance of you and your horse. At the other end of the scale, at the World Equestrian Games, medleys of popular music by performers such as Elvis Presley and Elton John were purely instrumental. I remember years ago at Goodwood Jane Bartle-Wilson riding her horse Pinnochio in the Grand Prix to nursery rhymes, complete with vocals, ticking clocks and so on, and it was a fantastic performance, great fun, and very popular with the audience.

The music should have clear changes of mood where it would be suitable to ride a different movement. When selecting tracks, try to listen for pieces of the music that could be cut to the right length of time required to make up your test from walk, trot and canter. This is easier to do with music that has clear phrases, with slight pauses between each, rather than music which slurs together, such as Scottish and Irish music. Irish music can sound fantastic to ride to, but it can be tricky picking out a section long enough that does not speed up, such as *Riverdance*, otherwise you will be going around like the clappers. 'Zorba the Greek' is another piece with a slow beginning and a very fast ending! (Joining pieces of such music to other tracks requires some technical skills – see Chapter 4 for more information.)

The technical aspect of choosing suitable music for your horse comes down to 'beats per minute'. This can sound daunting, but I do not think initially that you have to worry about it too much – just select music by riding to different tracks. However, if you feel the need to get technical, you need to arm yourself with a stopwatch. You will also need a willing assistant to time your horse as you lunge or ride him. If they time you for 15 seconds, and count how many footsteps your horse takes in that time, then multiply it by 4, this gives you the beats per minute of the walk, trot and canter. It is just the same as taking someone's pulse. Write it down and you should end up with a list such as:

Walk   100 beats per minute

Trot   140 beats per minute

Canter 100 beats per minute

This is actually my horse Heinrich's speed of rhythm (tempo).

Armed with this information, you may be lucky and find music which states beats per minute, but this is usually found only on CDs made specifically for riding to music. You can then sit at home in the luxury of your armchair, armed with your stopwatch, and time the beats per minute of different tracks to find suitable music. If the tempo matches that of your horse, then it should be easy to ride to.

If you want to be really clever, you could use a metronome, a measure of the beats per minute, which you can purchase from a music shop. This cuts out the need for the stopwatch, as you set the arm to swing in time with your horse's stride. Note the beats per minute, then at home set the metronome at the same speed, play different tracks and, if they fit the metronome beat, the music should be suitable. Personally, I have just used the 'listen and ride' technique, and used the stopwatch if I have been planning something very specific.

The Artistic Element

Deciding on a theme which suits your horse helps with the artistic element, for which you get half the marks allotted for the test. The other half are for technical execution, i.e. how well the movements are ridden (see Chapter 5). Humour works well – I remember a great little routine performed by two black cobs who were ridden to 'Love and Marriage', one wearing a top hat behind his ears and the other a wedding veil! The routine just contained walk and trot, and simple movements, but the rhythm of the music fitted so well with the horses. The riders were dressed simply in black and white.

In dressage to music competitions without costumes you need to bring out the combined personalities of you and your horse through your music and choice of movements (see next chapter), which comes under 'harmony between rider and horse'. Your choice of music will affect the choreography, i.e. how easy is it to fit the movements to the music. Marks are given for inventiveness, use of the arena, and choreography, so your music needs to allow you scope to do this. If the music is bland, you will end up just riding around to the same tune with no variation, which could become dull. If, on the other hand, the music has a lot of quick changes in it, it can sound choppy, and will not give you time to complete recognizable movements (such as not having time to do a whole circle), and the programme you ride will end up looking hectic. The music should allow you to keep the rhythm and energy flowing throughout the routine.

ENTRY MUSIC

Though this is not compulsory, it can add to the artistic element if you have an introduction. If you do not have a suitable fanfare which finishes at your first halt, you could ride what I call a 'flying start' where you start your walk, trot or canter music 20 seconds early, fade it for 4 seconds to allow for the halt and salute, and then continue in your chosen gait. This will then dictate which gait to start with when designing the routine (see next chapter). If you are lucky, you may find an introduction to a piece of music with a natural pause during which you could halt, salute and move off again.

3

CHOREOGRAPHY

*D*esigning a routine does not need to be complicated – the best advice is to keep it simple. Clever use of accurate circles, straight lines and other basic school movements such as serpentines and shallow loops can create the most wonderful patterns. Drawing them on a piece of paper can be a good starting point to make sure you use all the arena, and do the same movements on each rein.

Each level of competition states compulsory movements which must be included. The clever use of simple movements is rewarded in the artistic section of the marks given. As the artistic marks are half of the final total, it is worth putting as much effort as you can into riding a good test.

Compulsory and Optional Movements

For riders competing in the UK (or elsewhere under British Dressage rules) current test sheets at all levels are available from British Dressage, National Agricultural Centre, Stoneleigh Park, Kenilworth, Warwickshire CV8 2RJ. These give a list of compulsory movements. Optional movements are any movements up to and including those in the level of test being ridden. Riders competing in other countries will find that relevant tests sheets and lists of movements are available from their national organizing bodies, some of which are listed in the Appendix. The movements listed in this book are British Dressage movements current at the time of writing, but the tests are reviewed from time to time (a comment that applies to most national bodies), so do check the latest requirements before planning your choreography. Though the movements

DRESSAGE LEVELS

Dressage tests are compiled and listed in levels. Although the names of these levels vary from country to country, they all follow a broadly similar pattern of progression. Examples from a few countries (starting with the easiest level) are:

AUSTRALIA: Prep, Preliminary, Novice, Elementary, Medium, Advanced.

GERMANY: Klasse A, Klasse L, Klasse M, Klasse S.

UK: Preliminary, Novice, Elementary, Medium, Advanced Medium, Advanced.

USA: Introductory, Training, First, Second, Third, Fourth.

Note that the same, or similar-sounding, terms may sometimes be used by different national organizing bodies (e.g. of Australia and UK) to describe levels that do not actually equate with one another.

The FEI (Fédération Equestre Internationale) – the governing body of most equestrian sports, produces a series of Advanced level tests used, for instance, at international competitions and generally run under FEI rules. These tests, in ascending order, are: Prix St Georges, Intermediare I, Intermediare II, Grand Prix.

listed in the tests in this chapter are specific to British Dressage requirements, the practice exercises in which they are used are valuable to all dressage riders, wherever they might live, ride, and compete. I encourage you to take the time to study the sample tests I've provided – you can use them as 'worksheets' and fill in your country's compulsory and optional movements where appropriate. You'll find that following my recommended progression when designing your own freestyle teaches you how to use the arena optimally, segue smoothly from movement to movement, and eventually learn what works, and what doesn't in both practice and competition.

Me on the Friesian stallion, Darco – timing the movements is very important, even simple manoeuvres such as changing the diagonal.

The use of optional movements is rewarded in the artistic section of the test sheet. These should be of the standard of training required at the level of the test. For example, if you are competing at Novice level, movements should be used that are allowed at that level (see Designing a Novice Level Test later this chapter). If you throw in a half-pass or two, which are not allowed until Medium level, you will be penalized by two points each time you ride one!

There must be a halt at the beginning and end of the test, which must be on the centre line facing the judge. It could be very embarrassing if you end up facing the wrong way – I did it once, and suddenly realized I was doing my test upside down, heading up the centre line away from the judge with the end of the music looming, so I had to do a quick half-circle to turn around and head back again to the final halt! This the beauty of Freestyle tests – if you do make a mistake, you can get out of trouble if you think quickly. Amadeus is one for adapting the test to suit himself and sticking in the odd movement if I have not got his full attention. If he does this in a conventional test this causes problems and loses us marks – for example in the Prix St Georges he has been known to put in two-time changes at canter instead of threes. He has also managed to put in a couple of one-time changes coming out of a canter pirouette – very flash, but not in the test! He fares much better in Freestyle tests, and we often get good marks for choreography. I remember once turning down the centre line far too early: I could feel that Amadeus was thinking 'Yippee, she's lost it – let's have a spook', so we put in a canter half-pirouette going back on ourselves, then another to bring us towards the judge again for the final halt. The judge's comments were, 'Interesting pattern of movements'.

There are two ways of choreographing a test; working out the music first, and then fitting the movements to it, or working out the movements first, and choosing music to fit.

Fitting Movements to the Music

Personally, I compile the music first, making sure that the walk, trot and canter music selected is the correct length in total, i.e. between $4^1/_2$ and 5 minutes for a Novice test. If you are using entry music, listen to it carefully and decide whether to enter in walk, trot or canter. If you are using part of your walk, trot or canter music for a 'flying start' (see Chapter 2), this will dictate which gait you will be starting your routine with. Once I have the music sorted out, I ride to it, trying out different movements from the patterns on paper to see which fit the best.

You need several options at this stage, as what can look good on paper may either take too long to ride, or be too short and need padding out.

Listen to your music for hours on end until you know it by heart. Play it until you are almost fed up with it – then you know it! Try to recognize the sections of music, i.e. the verse and the chorus. This applies whether or not you have vocals. Listen for repetition of a phrase of music. Try to work out the routine so that you repeat a movement with the corresponding piece of music, for example, two loud pieces of trot music might correspond to two diagonals in medium trot. A 10 m circle on each rein would fit to eight beats of the music (two bars of four beats) twice in the routine. If you have four bits the same, you could do four 10 m circles, and so on. A longer piece of music may suit a three- or four-loop serpentine, or a 20 m circle on each rein. You do not have to work to the arena letters in Freestyle, but it does help to use them in planning out the evenness and balance of the movements you choose, so you do not end up with all the fancy bits on one side. The judge does not know your floor plan in advance, so has no idea of your intentions, but your movements must be recognizable, and the routine balanced on each rein. If you are aiming at a specific point in the arena, make it clear for the judge to see, otherwise your programme may appear vague, which could affect your marks.

PROCEDURE FOR ENTRY MUSIC

Entry music is not compulsory, and you do not get a mark for it separately, but it can add to the 'artistic impression' of the whole routine. If you are not using any, once the judge has signalled you to begin, head for your starting position on the centre line, halt, and raise one hand high to indicate that you wish the music to commence. Salute the judge and then proceed with your test.

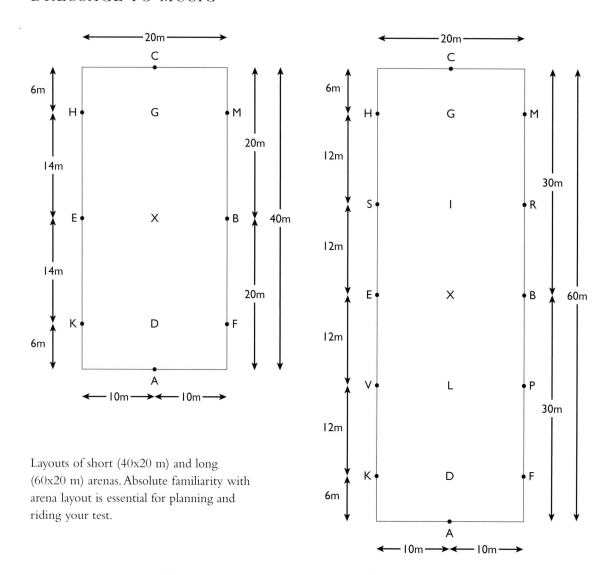

Layouts of short (40x20 m) and long (60x20 m) arenas. Absolute familiarity with arena layout is essential for planning and riding your test.

If you are using entry music, it must be no longer than 20 seconds, so you need to rehearse your entry beforehand so you know exactly where to begin. If you position yourself wrongly for the length of music, your first halt will not be where you planned it and this could throw your whole routine out of kilter. An example of correct procedure would be as follows. Position yourself in halt on the outside of the arena by the letter P, signal for your music to start and proceed in trot down the centre line. The music should end (or fade, if you are doing a 'flying start') as you perform the first halt of your routine, which indicates to the judge the point at which to begin marking the test. Allow 4 seconds for this halt and salute before proceeding with the routine proper.

Designing a Novice Level Test

Compulsory movements required at Novice level are:

Medium walk (minimum 20 m per movement)

Free walk on a long rein (minimum 20 m per movement)

Working trot left including a circle 15 m diameter

Working trot right including a circle 15 m diameter

Some medium trot strides

Working canter left including circle 20 m diameter

Working canter right including circle 20 m diameter

Optional movements at Novice level are:

Half- or full 10 m circles in walk or trot

Right and left turns

Rein-back

Some medium canter strides

Counter-canter

Give and retake the reins

Transitions, i.e. walk to trot, trot to canter. Walk to canter transitions are allowed but you may show a couple of trot steps (i.e. progressive) into canter.

Change of canter lead through trot

Serpentines of up to four loops

Single loops from the long side up to 10 m

20 m half-circles

SAMPLE NOVICE LEVEL TEST (20x40 M ARENA)

The following suggestion is for a 20x40 m arena allowing 2 minutes of trot work, 42 seconds of walk including medium and free walk, and 2 minutes 12 seconds of canter music – 4 minutes 54 seconds in total. Let's say you are starting with trot music, so you need to add on about 24 seconds extra to give you enough time to include a 4 second halt and salute and a 'flying start' (see Chapter 2), which leaves a bit of leeway in case you either come in a bit too 'gung-ho', or scared to death. Listen for a quiet bit which indicates your halt and salute – do not worry if it is not quite where you thought it would be – just listen to the music and it will tell you when to halt.

1. Enter the arena at A in trot, halt and salute at D. Proceed in working trot towards the track at H (i.e. incline DH).
2. Ride a 15 m circle at C, change the rein across the diagonal MK and show some medium trot strides.
3. Ride another 15 m circle at A (working trot).
4. Follow this with a three-loop serpentine, adding a circle in each of the loops. (The last one can be omitted if you get behind the music – remember, the judge doesn't know your intention beforehand.)
5. Your walk music comes next. Ride your transition to walk between C and H, ride medium walk from H to B, then free walk on a long rein from B to K. Finish the walk section with medium walk to A in preparation for a trot transition at A.
6. Canter at F, and then ride a 20 m circle left in working canter at B.
7. After the circle, continue around to C, ride a 20 m half-circle to X, change lead through trot, and ride another 20 m half-circle finishing at A.
8. Ride another 20 m circle in canter right from E, and continue around the arena to M.
9. Ride across the diagonal to K in medium canter.
10. At A ride a 20 m circle in working canter.
11. From F to H ride medium canter across the diagonal. Trot at H (or you could remain in canter, changing lead neatly before H if you wish.)
12. Proceed up the long side (either trot or canter), and turn down the centre line for the final halt and salute at X (allow 4 seconds).

You can see from the diagram that you have used the whole arena, and the programme looks well balanced, with work on both reins. It is simple, but has enough variety to make it interesting to watch. You do not want the poor judge – who has many tests to watch – to become bored, but on the other hand you do not want to make the test too confusing. The judge should be able to identify easily which movement you are doing at the time!

The test can be varied by starting with either the walk or canter sections. Beginning with canter works better for Elementary tests and upwards, bearing in mind that your start from the first halt is directly into canter – though this can be progressive at Elementary level.

Sample Novice Freestyle test for a 20x40 m arena.

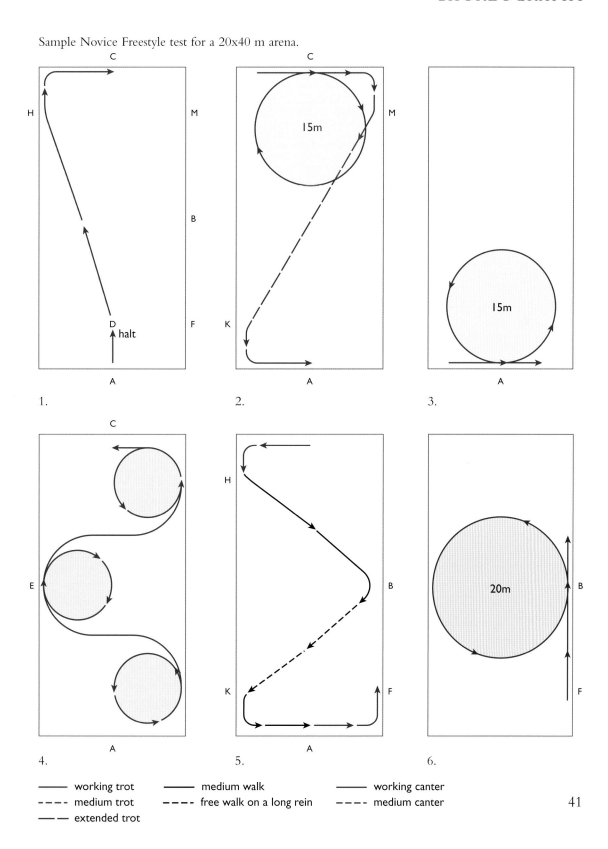

Continued.

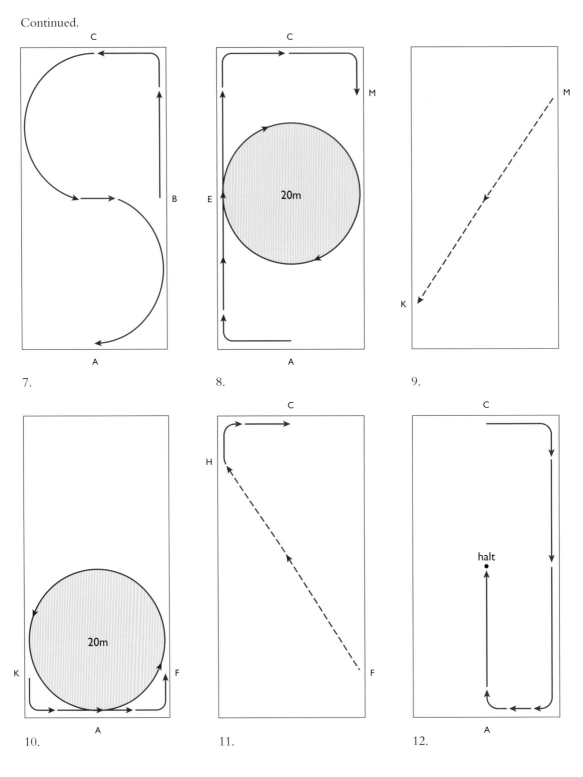

7.

8.

9.

10.

11.

12.

Designing an Elementary Level Test

Compulsory movements at Elementary level are:
Medium walk (minimum 20 m per movement)
Free walk on a long rein (minimum 20 m per movement)
Circle left in working trot 10 m diameter
Circle right in working trot 10 m diameter
Medium trot
Leg-yield left
Leg-yield right
Circle left in working canter 15 m diameter
Circle right in working canter 15 m diameter
Medium canter
Simple change left to right
Simple change right to left
(Downwards transitions to walk from canter can be progressive, i.e. through trot, but upward ones must be direct)

Optional movements at Elementary level are as Novice level, plus:
Large half-pirouettes in walk
Five-loop serpentine
8 m circles in trot
8 m half-circles in canter

SAMPLE ELEMENTARY LEVEL TEST
(20x60 M ARENA)

Try to put the compulsory movements in first, so you do not miss any out, and fill in any free time with additional movements, or repeat anything which did not go well the first time. For example, if your first medium trot was lacking in impulsion, and you feel you could improve it, do another one. If, however, you do not want to risk it, you could play safe and ride working trot, though you might have to adjust your floor plan by altering the size and shape of your corners. (When fitting your movements to music, you can do this as necessary: i.e. if you need to 'catch up' you can ride shallow corners; if you need to 'get ahead' you can rider deeper into the corners.)

1. Enter in medium walk, halt and salute at L. Proceed in free walk (flying start as in Novice test) on the short diagonal (LS) line to the long side; at the track ride a transition to medium walk, and proceed around the short side to M.

2. Make a transition into working trot, and ride a 10 m circle to the right at R. Turn across the arena between R and B, turn left and ride another 10 m circle, this time to the left at E. Proceed in medium trot across a diagonal line directly from E to the far end of the arena at F.

3. From A ride a four-loop serpentine finishing at C.

4. Proceed across the diagonal HP in medium trot, returning to working trot at P.

5. Turn down the centre line at A in working trot, leg-yield left to S, then proceed up the long side. Turn down the centre line at C, and ride leg-yield right back to the track at V.

6. Ride a transition to working canter at A, and immediately circle left 15 m diameter.

7. Ride medium canter across the diagonal from F to H, then a transition to working trot. Canter at C and ride a 15 m circle, then proceed around the school to R.

8. At R, turn across the school to S with a simple change of leg (through walk) on the centre line. Continue in working canter around the arena to P.

9. At P, turn across the arena to V and ride a simple change on the centre line. At V, track right, and ride medium canter on the diagonal EM. Change lead through trot towards the end of the diagonal, with a transition to working canter at M.

10. Continue in working canter up the long side and ride a 10 m half-circle from V to the centre line. Continue down the centre line to the final halt at I.

Sample Elementary Freestyle test for a 20x60 m arena.

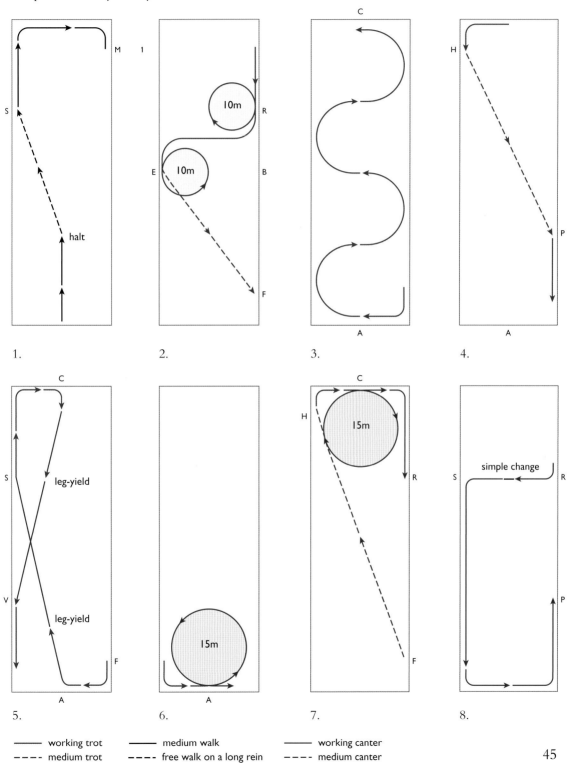

1.   2.   3.   4.

5.   6.   7.   8.

working trot	medium walk	working canter
medium trot	free walk on a long rein	medium canter

Continued.

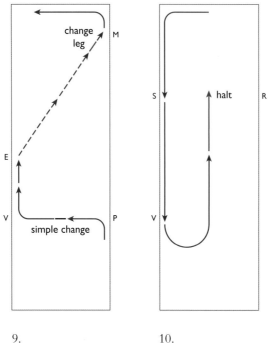

9.   10.

Designing a Medium Level Test

Compulsory **movements at Medium level are:**

Collected walk (minimum 20 m per movement)
Extended walk (minimum 20 m per movement)
Collected trot
Half-pass left in trot
Half-pass right in trot
Medium trot
Counter-canter left (minimum 20 m)
Counter-canter right (minimum 20 m)
Collected canter
Half-pass left in canter
Half-pass right in canter
Medium canter
Simple change left to right
Simple change right to left
Halts at beginning and end of test

Optional movements are:

Shoulder-in left

Shoulder-in right

Quarter- and half-pirouettes in walk

SAMPLE MEDIUM LEVEL TEST (20x60 M ARENA)

This routine is to Scottish music. The numbered movements correspond to those shown on the diagram. The movements are simple to help keep a flow to the test, which is especially important if your horse is new to this level. The letters are used as a guide to explain the movements. In this routine, the trot music is split into two sections – one at the beginning and the other at the end.

1. Start position at P. Introduction **Reel selection (20 seconds)**. Halt and salute. Music change to trot **In Reel Time (56 seconds)** down the centre line and halt at X. Proceed in collected trot.

2. Track left, and ride shoulder-in left to E. Change the rein by riding a 10 m half-circle to X, followed by a half-circle right to B. Ride shoulder-in right as far as F.

3. Change the rein across the diagonal KM in medium trot.

4. Music change to walk **Para Handy (46 seconds)**. At C ride a 20 m circle – the first half in collected walk, the second in extended walk.

5. Change to canter music **Linton Ploughman Jig (2 minutes 8 seconds)**. At C, ride a transition to collected canter left. Ride-half pass left across the arena to P, then staying in counter-canter, ride a 20 m half-circle to V. Ride a simple change (through walk).

6. Continue up the long side in medium canter to H. From M, ride half-pass right to V, then a 20 m half-circle in counter-canter to P, with a simple change at P.

7. Ride medium canter on the diagonal PH. At H, transition to collected canter.

8. Commencing at C, ride a four-loop serpentine with a simple change through walk each time you cross the centre line, finishing at A.

9. Music change to trot **In Reel Time (1 minute)**. Transition to collected trot at A. Ride half-pass left F to X. At X, ride a 10 m circle left, followed by half-pass right from X to M.

10. Continue around the arena, riding medium trot on the long side between H and K. Turn down the centre line at A and halt and salute at X.

DRESSAGE TO MUSIC

Sample Medium Freestyle test for a 20x60 m arena, as ridden to a selection of Scottish music.

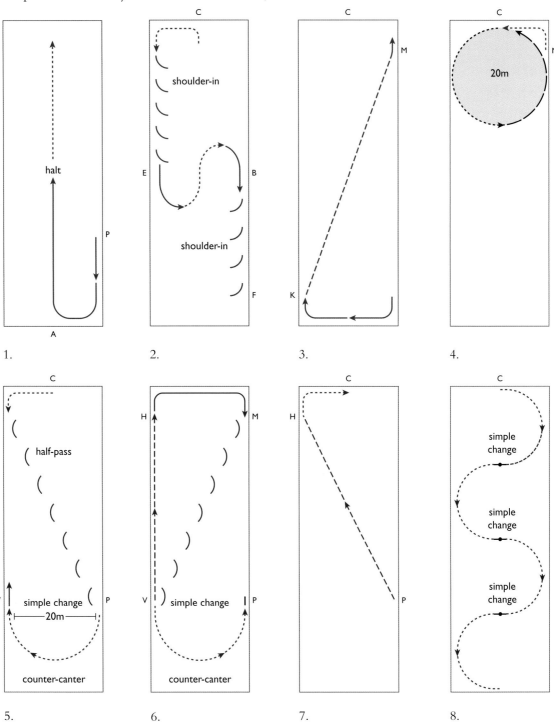

1.   2.   3.   4.

5.   6.   7.   8.

Continued.

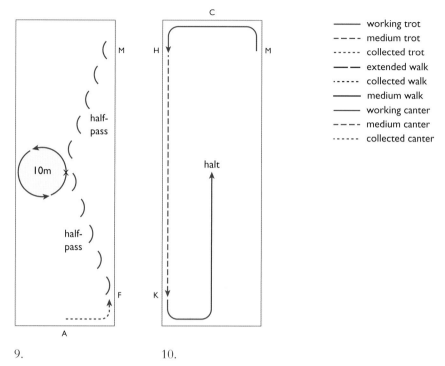

9.   10.

Designing an Advanced Medium Level Test

Compulsory movements at Advanced Medium level are:

Collected walk (minimum 20 m per movement)

Extended walk (minimum 20 m per movement)

Collected trot

Extended trot

Shoulder-in left

Shoulder-in right

Half-pass left

Half-pass right

Collected canter

Medium canter

One or more single flying changes right to left

One or more single flying changes left to right

Halts at beginning and end of test

Optional **movements at Advanced Medium level are:**

8 m circles in canter

Give and retake reins in collected canter

SAMPLE ADVANCED MEDIUM LEVEL TEST (20x60 M ARENA)

Here is a plan for a test at Advanced Medium level to Irish music from 'Lord of the Dance'. The numbered movements correspond to the diagram. The letters are used as a guide as to where you should be, but you can improvise as necessary, for example, by turning earlier off the track into the canter half-circles if you get behind, or adding in 10 m circles between the shoulder-in and half-pass in trot if you get ahead. The total length of the routine is 5 minutes, plus 20 seconds of introduction.

1. Starting position near F.

    Introduction 20 seconds in working trot to **'Lord of the Dance' (20 seconds)**. Halt near X.

    Music change to **'Gypsy' (2 minutes 5 seconds)**.

    Proceed in collected trot. At C track left, at H ride a 10 m circle right.

2. Trot the short diagonal HB, and next short diagonal BK. At F ride a 10 m circle left.

3. Ride shoulder-in left up the long side to B. Half-pass left to the centre line near G.

4. At C track left and change the rein across the long diagonal HF in extended trot. Collected trot at F.

5. At K, ride shoulder-in right up the long side to E, then half-pass right to the centre line near G.

6. Walk music **'Warriors' (43 seconds)**. At C track right and ride a two-loop serpentine finishing at X. Ride the first loop in collected walk, and the second in extended walk.

7. Canter music **'Siamsa' (2mins 12 seconds)**. Ride a transition to collected canter right at X, at B track right. Canter a 10 m half-circle at F, return to the track in half-pass right to B. Flying change at B.

8. Continue up the track to M, ride a 10 m half-circle left, and return to the track in half-pass left. Flying change at B. Proceed in collected canter around the arena to K, then ride medium canter up the long side to H. Transition to collected canter.

Sample Advanced Medium Freestyle test for a 20x60 m arena, as ridden to music from 'Lord of the Dance'.

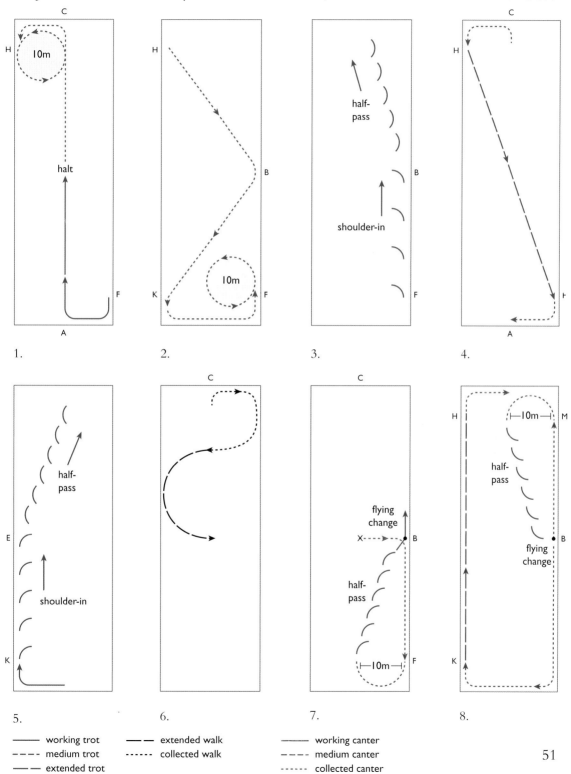

Continued.

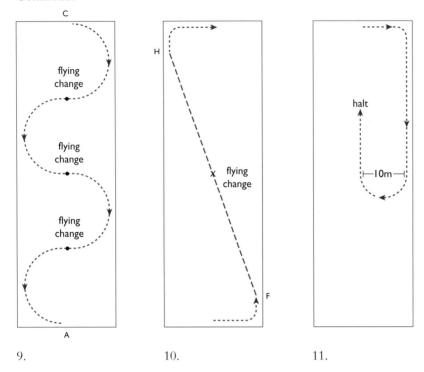

9.   10.   11.

9. Ride a four-loop serpentine starting at C and finishing at A with a flying change each time you cross the centre line.

10. Ride medium canter across the diagonal FH, with a flying change at X and a transition to collected canter at H.

11. Canter around the arena, turning off the track, with a 10 m half-circle right, to the centre line. You have a bit of leeway here to turn appropriately to get you to your final halt at I by the end of the music.

Movements for FEI Level Tests

PRIX ST GEORGES LEVEL
(FEI YOUNG RIDERS TEST)
Compulsory movements at **Prix St Georges level are:**
Collected walk (minimum 20 m per movement)
Extended walk (minimum 20 m per movement) – a coefficient of 2 is applied★
Collected trot including shoulder-in right

Collected trot including shoulder-in left
Collected trot including half-pass right – a coefficient of 2 is applied★
Collected trot including half-pass left – a coefficient of 2 is applied★
Extended trot
Collected canter
Collected canter including half-pass right
Collected canter including half-pass left
Extended canter
Flying changes every fourth stride (minimum 5 times consecutively)
Flying changes every third stride (minimum 5 times consecutively)
Half-pirouette in canter right – a coefficient of 2 is applied★
Half-pirouette in canter left – a coefficient of 2 is applied★

★*Where coefficients of 2 apply, marks given for the movement are doubled*

Optional **movements at Prix St Georges level are:**
Travers
Renvers

INTERMEDIARE I LEVEL TEST

Compulsory **movements at Intermediare I level are:**
Collected walk (minimum 20 m per movement)
Extended walk (minimum 20 m per movement) – a coefficient of 2 is applied★
Collected trot including shoulder-in right
Collected trot including shoulder-in left
Collected trot including half-pass right – a coefficient of 2 is applied★
Collected trot including half-pass left – a coefficient of 2 is applied★
Extended trot
Collected canter
Collected canter including half-pass right
Collected canter including half-pass left
Extended canter
Flying changes every third stride (minimum 5 times consecutively)
Flying changes every second stride (minimum 5 times consecutively)
Single pirouette in canter right – a coefficient of 2 is applied★
Single pirouette in canter left – a coefficient of 2 is applied★

★*Where coefficients of 2 apply, marks given for the movement are doubled*

Optional **movements for Intermediare I level are:**

Travers

Renvers

Half-pirouettes

GRAND PRIX LEVEL

Compulsory **movements at Grand Prix level are:**

Collected walk (minimum 20 m per movement)

Extended walk (minimum 20 m per movement)

Collected trot including half-pass right

Collected trot including half-pass left

Extended trot

Collected canter

Collected canter including half-pass right

Collected canter including half-pass left

Extended canter

Flying changes every second stride (minimum 5 times consecutively)

Flying changes every stride (minimum 9 times consecutively)

Single pirouette in canter right – a coefficient of 2 is applied★

Single pirouette in canter left – a coefficient of 2 is applied★

Passage (minimum 20 m: on one track) – a coefficient of 2 is applied★

Piaffe (minimum 10 steps straight) – a coefficient of 2 is applied★

Transitions from passage to piaffe and from piaffe to passage – a coefficient of 2 is applied★

★Where coefficients of 2 apply, marks given for the movement are doubled

Optional **movements for Grand Prix level:**

At this level, optional movements can be combination movements such as double pirouettes in canter or half-pass in passage, which can add to the artistic element of the test, but do not contribute to the technical aspect. Your test should primarily be technically correct and uphold the principles of dressage, and not degenerate into 'tricks'. (See Chapter 5 Technical Execution for further details.)

I remember judging a Spanish Advanced Freestyle test in which any movement was allowed – including Spanish walk and airs above the ground such as levade – which was quite an experience. The test sheet was just a list of all the movements; the difficulty was recognizing what was being performed in front of my eyes. It took a great deal of concentration and speed of decision to give the marks. The best tests were easy to follow and had a clear pattern of selected movements which suited the horse but some tests, in which the rider had just tried to pack in as much as possible, aiming for quantity rather than quality, were rather confusing.

Work Out the Routine First

Working out the routine first requires timing each movement you wish to ride, then fitting them together to the required length of test. For this method, you will need a willing helper with a stopwatch, or film of your horse performing each of the movements individually. For example, time how long it takes to ride the long diagonal in working trot, or how long it takes to canter a 20 m circle. The movements could be filmed/timed at the same time you are working out the 'beats per minute' when selecting the music to fit the gaits (see Chapter 2). This takes time but, if you write it all down, you then have a reference for the next test you choreograph and will not have to do it all again – unless, of course, you horse's gaits change and develop through his training. His rhythm may well become slower as he takes bigger, more powerful steps and he may cover more ground, which will affect the timing of each movement!

The diagram overleaf shows approximate timings for several movements. You can see how useful it would be to keep a record of each movement on file ready for each test you design! Even if the timings are just approximate, you will get some idea of how many movements you can fit into a test.

Note how many steps your horse takes to perform circles and corners, as this can help you to keep in time with the music: for instance, if it takes eight strides in working trot to do a 10 m circle, that should fit to two bars of music if it is four beats to a bar, and you can ensure that all your 10 m circles are the correct size. If you get round one of them in six strides, either it is too small, or your length of stride in trot has changed! When riding a turn across the school I usually allow six steps, whether I am in walk, trot or canter: two steps to prepare, two steps to turn, and two steps afterwards. I ride corners as quarter circles, again allowing six steps. If it takes 4 seconds to ride a corner, then your music needs six beats to every 4 seconds to fit exactly!

Timing of movements.

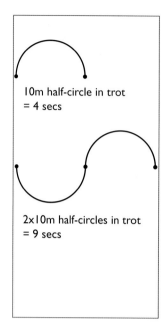

1.

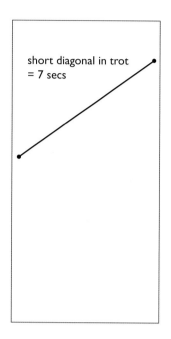

2.

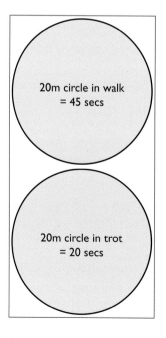

3.

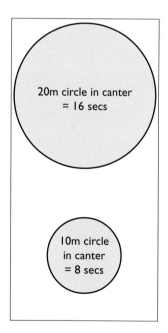

4.

Doing your choreography like this can be quite time-consuming, and requires some dedication, but it gives you the option to make a more complicated routine with frequent changes between gaits if you wish, i.e. a diagonal in medium trot, followed by a 10 m circle in canter, then returning to trot again. This is worth doing if you have reached the higher echelons of competition and are aiming for the top, such as the European Championships or the Olympic Games, where you could have music composed specifically to fit your routine. If you want to do this, there are several companies that will make a music track to fit a video of you and your horse performing the test you have designed. These may be found on the internet, or it may be worth approaching a local sound studio that may do it for you.

If you are attempting a test at a new level, or just starting out, keep the choreography fairly simple, so as not to interrupt the flow of the test, especially if your horse is prone to becoming a bit tense. Whirling him around too much may not allow him to settle into the all-important rhythm. As you become more confident, then the routine can be added to in the future.

CUEING MOVEMENTS

You will need to pick key words or phrases in the music to cue the movements. I have used the *Mary Poppins* medley originally designed for the Quadrille at Olympia (see Chapter 9), revamped to fit the requirements for Prix St Georges level. You obviously need to be very familiar with the tracks for this to make full sense, but this is an example of how the process works. Overleaf is a reproduction of the actual working sheet that I carry about with me to competitions. The key words are in bold text in brackets.

You can see from my notes that I pinpoint key letters where I must end up, and words to listen out for to give me clues as to where I should be at any given time. I leave myself 'room to manoeuvre' during the movements.

Another example of cueing movements comes from what I call my Egyptian routine. I rode this routine at an X Factor dressage charity event. The inspiration behind the theme of the performance was a holiday I had taken in Egypt. The costume was an authentic Belly Dancer's outfit bought from the Bazaar in Cairo (with a lot of price haggling!) and it is great to ride in. The skirt is split at the front and sides, with a large rear panel which enables it to hang well over the horse's back. The material is heavy enough not to float about too much, and the waist belt, complete with 'authentic'

SAMPLE TEST AT PRIX ST GEORGES LEVEL RIDDEN TO MARY POPPINS

Entrance Music

1. Enter collected canter.

   X halt, salute.

   Proceed collected walk. Half-pirouette left (snap).

   Go back up the centre line, pirouette right (finish on 'that's a…').

'Spoonful of Sugar'

2. 'Spoonful' collected canter right, turn right.

   Half-pass right to X, 10 m circle, ('feathering his nest') continue in half-pass.

3. At A ('twig') flying change, next diagonal half-pass left to X.

   10 m half-circle left followed by 20 m half-circle in medium canter (whooshing music).

4. Continue in half-pass to corner, flying change at C. Music change.

'Jolly Holiday'

5. Working up the quarter lines in collected trot go with four-beat music ('big bass drum') medium trot a few steps, working up school ride shoulder-in right, half-circles right and left to change rein, shoulder-in left, half-circles left and right, travers right, half-circles again, travers left. Finish at A.

'Chim Chiminee'

6. Extended walk two big loops slalom up centre line. At X collected trot, half-pass left and right finish at C left rein.

7. Long side – shallow loop in extended canter.

'Supercalifrag…'

8. Diagonal four-time changes (five in succession).

9. Diagonal three-time changes (five in succession).

10. Short diagonal into canter half-pirouette left, (Mary Poppins talking).

11. Half-pirouette right (man talking) finishing at A.

12. Collected canter towards G. Halt and salute.

Sample Prix St Georges Freestyle test for a 20x60 m arena, as ridden to *Mary Poppins*.

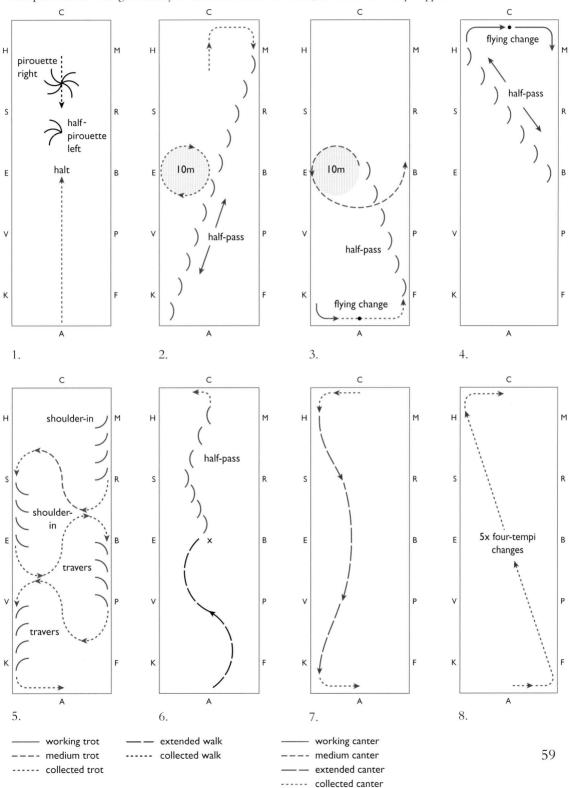

Continued.

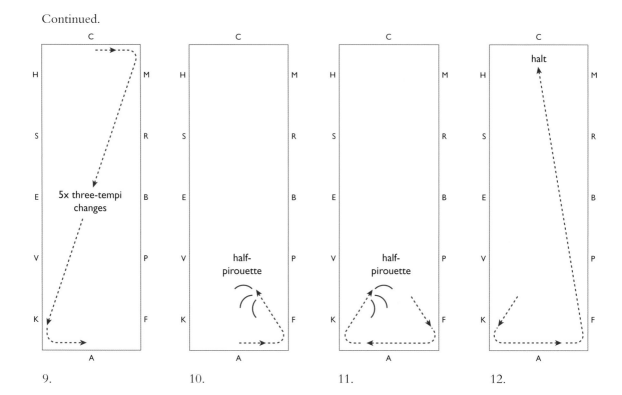

9.   10.   11.   12.

coins, produces a great jangling sound during movement. We had to have a dress rehearsal, though, to accustom Amadeus to the noise and to me appearing draped in bright scarlet from head to toe! He was quite taken with the breast-plate, as the tassels bounced around, brushing him on the chest, so we achieved better 'lightness of the forehand' than usual. The outfit certainly caught the interest of passers-by. Our arena is close to a road, so we heard squealing brakes as passing vehicles stopped to peer at this strange apparition in the Wiltshire countryside. I waved and carried on, and Amadeus showed off (as he does) once he realized that he was the centre of attention.

I had fancied riding to the classical music, 'Scheherazade', but it did not suit Amadeus at all. The music was finally selected in our local pub with the help of our friends who are musically inclined and have a wealth of knowledge on 1980s pop music! I knew the tunes I wanted, but did not know the titles of the tracks or the artists, so we spent an enjoyable evening trying to remember them! We came up with 'Night Boat to Cairo' by Madness for the trot and 'Walk Like an Egyptian' by the Bangles for the walk. The canter music, 'Egyptian Reggae', was quite repetitive, but it fitted

Amadeus's canter so well that I just had to use it. I interspersed it with some short bursts of authentic belly dancing music so I could time the movements more easily and hopefully complete each section at the correct point in the arena. I did try riding all the three gaits to belly dancing music, but there are only so many minutes of 'bongos' one can take at a time without it sounding monotonous, so I went for the 'fun factor', using zigzags to represent 'going up the River Nile' and canter pirouettes to represent 'dancing the night away'.

A dress rehearsal without the final 'bling' to accustom Amadeus to his breast-plate and to the red apparition in the saddle.

The reprise of the routine that was read out by the commentator to 'set the scene' was as follows:

Arabian Nights – Scheherazade's Tale

Our Princess has to flee the Sultan's palace to avoid having her head chopped off. She catches the 'Night Boat to Cairo', crosses the desert 'Walking like an Egyptian', where she meets her lover and dances the night away to Egyptian Reggae.

The routine goes as follows (the music chosen is highlighted in bold):

1. Introduction (**belly dancing music – drums and cymbals**) starting on the outside of the arena boards from B, enter arena at A in medium canter, halt at X.

   'Night Boat to Cairo'. Proceed in collected trot, at C turn left and ride shoulder-in left up the long side to E.

2. Change the rein by riding a 10 m half-circle circle left to X, followed by a 10 m circle right to the track at B. Proceed in shoulder-in right up the long side to the quarter marker.

3. Turn down the centre line at A and ride a half-pass zigzag (key words **'up the River Nile'**).

4. At C turn right, and extended trot up the long side to instrumental bit.

5. Keep going across the diagonal to just before X. Music slows so ride a few steps of passage. As music gets louder, resume extended trot with transitions to collected trot, and then walk as the music fades.

DRESSAGE TO MUSIC

Freestyle 'Egyptian theme' test as ridden for a charity event.

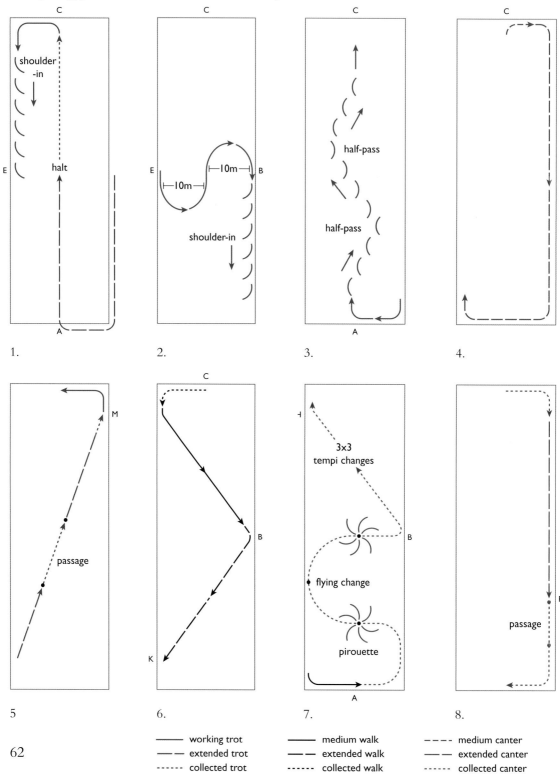

1. shoulder-in · halt · C · E · A

2. shoulder-in · 10m · 10m · C · E · B

3. half-pass · half-pass · C · A

4. C

5. passage · M

6. C · B · K

7. 3x3 tempi changes · flying change · pirouette · C · B · A

8. passage · C · P

— working trot   — medium walk   --- medium canter

— — extended trot   — — extended walk   — — extended canter

····· collected trot   ····· collected walk   ····· collected canter

6. Music changes to '**Walk like an Egyptian**'. Ride collected walk from C to the corner, medium walk across the short diagonal to B. Ride extended walk on the short diagonal from B to K.

7. Music changes to '**Egyptian Reggae**'. Ride collected canter from A. Ride a two-loop serpentine to X. Crossing the centre line for the first time, ride a full canter pirouette to the left. Ride a flying change at the track at V, then a pirouette right crossing the centre line for the second time (at X). Proceed to B, and ride 3x three-tempi changes on the short diagonal to H.

8. Ride extended canter up the long side. This should change to passage at P when you hear the '**bongo drums**' for 10 seconds.

9. After '**bongo drums**' collected canter up the centre line from A, riding a zigzag in canter half-pass finishing at C.

10. At C turn right, and passage to the '**bongo drums**' (another check point!) Canter with two-tempi changes up the long side, and head towards G in collected canter for the final halt and salute with the end of the music.

Continued.

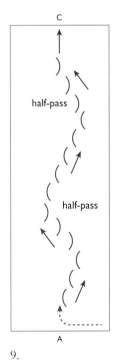

9.

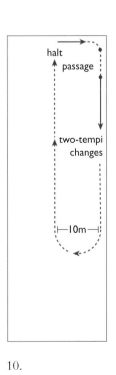

10.

Performing under the spotlights – Amadeus actually listened to me on this occasion.

4

CREATING THE MUSIC TRACK – THE TECHNICALITIES

*B*y now you should have been riding to music in your school, and have selected suitable walk, trot and canter music. The next stage is to put the music together and fit it to the length required for your test. The time required for Novice, Elementary, Medium, Advanced Medium, Prix St Georges and Intermediare I levels is $4^1/_2$–5 minutes; at Grand Prix level it is $5^1/_2$–6 minutes.

You may add to the time an introduction for your entry into the arena before the first halt: this introduction should be no longer than 20 seconds at the time of writing. The test is timed from the move-off after the first salute until the halt before the final salute. Two penalty points will be deducted from the final total if a test exceeds the maximum time allowed or is 30 seconds shorter than the minimum time. The music may start either before the entry at A or after the first halt and salute. Any faults in the reproduction of the music will be taken into account by the judge and will affect the score for 'Music and interpretation of the music'. Judges have the authority to restart a competitor should the music fail to start. This happened to me when CDs were first introduced. I thought I had been very clever and made my own music CD on my computer, only to find that the elderly machine at the competition did not recognize it, so nothing happened! Fortunately, I had a tape of the music in the jeep, so a kind person fetched it for me and we started again. I now always take my music on both CD and tape just in case it should ever happen again.

Recording from CDs to Cassette Tape

Cassette tapes are pretty 'old hat' these days, and more and more competition venues are now only accepting CDs, so it is worth checking whether a particular venue has a facility for playing cassette tapes before you spend hours with your finger on the button, so to speak! However, some people may still wish to use cassettes, at least for 'back up', for the reasons just given above, so I felt explaining the process worthwhile.

Creating a suitable music track can be done easily at home on your stereo, if you still have a music system with which you can record from CD to cassette tape. If you have a fader button which allows you to fade each track in and out where you want to join them, this can be a great help and avoids strange clicks and jumps in the music. Failing that, if you are recording onto a cassette, you have to be quick on the pause button to stop music at a suitable point; this enables you to join the next track without any strange clicks or wailing noises. (This method has served me well for twenty years – I still use the same machine!) The trick is to listen to each piece of music several times over. If your music system has a counter (i.e. as each track plays it starts at zero and counts each second), it helps you to pinpoint where you need to 'pause' or 'play'. It is better to use the pause button before you hit the stop button, to avoid clicks. If you are recording onto a tape, use good quality tapes, and if you have the option of recording at a loud volume, do so. If your recording is quiet the volume will need to be turned up high on the player at the competition, which may lead to distortion and may affect your artistic mark for your music.

Make sure that you use a blank tape for your final test copy. Sometimes it is easy to record over and over again onto the same tape, resulting in odd bits of music at the beginning and end, so make sure you either wipe the tape completely or use a new one. Wind the tape forwards slightly to the brown tape before you start recording onto it, so you do not accidentally lose a bit of your routine by recording over the white bit of tape at the beginning of the spool.

Burning CDs on Your Computer

The internet is a great source of information, offering CDs of suitable music to ride to which give you the beats per minute for each track. Match the tracks that fit to your horse's beats per minute for his walk, trot and canter. On average, walk and canter have the same beats per minute, ranging from 85 to 115 steps per minute, and trot tends to range between 125 and 160 steps per minute. If you are planning music for more than one horse (e.g. for a Pas de Deux or Quadrille), you need to chose an average frequency so that both/all can manage – for example about 140 steps per minute for the trot. Then it comes down to horsemanship and riders being able to regulate their horses' gaits to the music. The alternative is to use any music that you like that you have tried out with your horse and find easy to ride to. It is easy to download music tracks and to save them on your computer.

The next step is to select a section of each track to build up your routine, for example 2 minutes of trot, 45 seconds of walk and 2 minutes of canter, plus 20 seconds of entry music (see Chapter 2.). You will need a CD editing programme to do this if you want to do it yourself, but the results can be of very good quality and perfectly suitable for playing at full volume. It is best to choose music from the same CD so the sound and quality of track match. You will need to import your music into your computer so that you can edit it. Save the file as a WAV file, so that it can be played on most types of CD player. MP3 files are not recognized by 'old-fashioned' CD players, as I have found out to my cost! If you are recording from an old film track, for example, the original quality of the recording may sound okay at home, but poor when played at full volume at a competition.

Me at work on the computer.

If you need to alter the speed of the music, this requires more sophisticated software, and more time to understand the instructions, so you could spend hours working it out, but once you have cracked it, you should be fine. (However, if you have a track with vocals, these may become distorted, so instrumental music is the better choice if you need to tinker with speed.) Mind you, this is beyond the realms of my own computer literacy, so I just ride in time with the music I end up with! You can create your own music using some software, which turns your keyboard and mouse into 'virtual instruments', but you do need some musical talent for this, though the possibilities are endless.

Using Sound Studios

Using the services of the local sound studio does not have to be expensive. They can join together your selected music probably more quickly and seamlessly than you could do at home, for a professional finish. Work out the tracks you want, and how much of each, and the studio can join them together for you. This is even quicker if you know precisely which bits of music you want. For example, if your trot music has a nice booming section 3 minutes in which would fit a medium trot, which you would like to ride at end of your trot section, then chose 2 minutes of trot finishing with the loud bit. You would have to inform the sound technician where to start and finish the trot music. A sample music plan could be as follows.

Scottish Dance Bands

Gait	Track	Title	Start	Finish	Length of Music
Intro	Track 16	Reel selection	0 min 0 secs	20 secs, 4 secs gap – halt	20 secs 4 secs
Trot music	Track 7	In Reel Time	1 min 30 secs	3 min 30 secs	2 minutes
Walk music	Track 14	Para Handy	1 min 15 secs	2 minutes	45 secs
Canter music	Track	Linton Jig	45 secs	End of track	2 minutes 8 secs
		Total (inc. Intro.)			5 minutes 17 secs

It is easier if you are present during the studio session, so you can answer any questions, and check the final CD before you leave. The technician can match the sound levels of each track so that the volume is the same all the way through. There is nothing worse than your music starting off loudly, so the person on DJ duty turns the volume down, only to find that the rest of your music is too quiet. You will be straining to hear it, and may lose your cues. The judge(s) will also not get the full benefit of your music. The sound studio can also make sure that the sound quality of your CD is good enough to be played loudly in an arena, especially if it is outdoors. Poor recordings can sound muffled and clarity can be lost. The music could also sound 'tinny' and thin.

Specially Composed Music

You could send a film of your horse in walk, trot and canter to an internet company offering to compose music for you, so you have a complete track, blending the three gaits together in an especially composed piece of music. If you do not have the facilities to have a video made of you and your horse, you could send a list stating how long you want of each gait, and what the beats per minute are, for your own personal composition to be made. Some companies will even help you to compile your test.

Ready-made CDs

Other companies on the internet offer ready-made music CDs of the required length, so all you have to do is to make up the movements to fit. This can be very useful if you are short of time. Another option is to send your CDs to the company for them to join together the tracks for you in the same way as the sound studio (see above). They will send you your music on a CD (and, sometimes, a tape), and will send you a download version via the internet so you can check it before the final CD is burned.

Another option is to have a music CD put together from music selected by the company, for which they need sufficient information from you about the amount of walk, trot and canter, beats per minute and any preferred types of music, to enable them to do this – or alternatively a video film of your test.

The disadvantage of using a company to do your music is that you may not have a unique routine. I have been at a competition where it was easy to pick out riders who had used the same company, as their music was very similar. There were a lot of Western theme tunes that afternoon! Music played on a synthesizer is commonly used and this can sound very 'samey', especially to a judge who has heard four tests sounding alike.

Selecting your own music has the advantage that you know your own horse's personality, and what will suit him best, and you can be fairly certain that you have a unique routine.

Using Live Musicians

If you have access to a band or group, or have a musical family member, you could ask them to compose something for you – but make sure that they can play the type of music you are after. They could compose something new for you, or they may make up a medley of 'cover versions' of well-known tunes. *Do* state that vocals are not required, otherwise you may get more than you bargained for. The band will need the beats per minute required for walk, trot and canter, and how long for. They may have never heard of dressage to music, so it may be worth sending them a short film, or inviting them to watch you ride your horse if they are local. The band will certainly want a fee for their trouble.

Practice Music

Whichever form of production you select for your music, it is important to make a practice version. Record the music several times over, so you can practice riding the routine without continually getting on and off your horse, or riding to your CD player and pressing 'play' over and over again. Leave a pause after each time you record it to give yourself time to get back to your starting position, otherwise you will keep missing your grand entrance, and be scrabbling to begin the routine. I take a practice tape and CD with me everywhere I go, and play the music over and over in the car to make sure I know it thoroughly. I usually have a piece of paper and pen handy also, to 'doodle' the test at every opportunity. Keeping a master CD at home is a good idea should you need to make a new copy at any time, whether to tape, CD, or a more modern, high-tech system. Also, you do not run the risk of losing your precious music.

Editing

Listen to the tracks you have chosen over and over again, and select which part of each track you re going to use. For the introduction, you may find a fanfare at the beginning of a piece of music, so this would be a good start. If you are very lucky, it will be the right length to get you to your starting point, but you may need to fade it at an appropriate point into the pause for the halt. Allow 4 seconds for the halt/salute. Too long, and the judge will be wondering if your music is going to play at all, and you may be anxious yourself! Too short a pause, and you will rush your salute, and be fumbling to pick up your reins again in time to move off.

Use the beginning of a piece of music for the move-off from halt to give a clear indication to the judge that you are under way. For example, if you moved off in trot, this piece can be faded into the next for the walk. The next piece of music could be faded in and out, but make sure that the last piece you use, for example your canter music, has a good finish to take you into a dramatic final halt. To achieve this, try using the last section of a piece of music so you finish when the music does, to give you a punchy end to your test. Sometimes, fading the music into halt can be just as effective, especially if you have had some dramatic moments in the rest of the music. The judge may appreciate a classy, controlled finish rather than a mad dash to the final halt with a slamming on of the brakes!

Music Licensing

The information given in this section is specific to UK law, and to arrangements with British Dressage. Laws relating to music licensing may also be in force in other countries, and riders competing outside the UK are advised to consult their national organizing body regarding procedure.

To play copied music in public in the UK, you must have a music licence. You can arrange this by completing and returning both a music sub-licence agreement and a music licence record form listing tracks, the artist and record label, which are available from British Dressage, Stoneleigh Park, Kenilworth, Warwickshire CV8 2RJ. They will supply you with sticky labels which you must complete and attach to your CD or other recording system to fulfil the licence agreement. This allows you to use any music from the record labels listed on the PPL list which they supply you with. It is a very long list, not of individual tracks but of recording labels, so just look on the tapes, CDs or whatever you are recording from to check which recording label they come under. If you have your music compiled by a professional company, they will make up a finished music track for you to use, and they will have listed the details for you. You must still complete the necessary paperwork for the British Dressage Office.

5

TECHNICAL EXECUTION

*R*iding movements accurately will increase your score for technical marks. There's no point having the best music selection if the riding of the movements is poor, as this will reflect on how the horse has been trained. Riding a dressage test should be an extension of the schooling you do at home. By concentrating on how your horse works, whether you are jumping, hacking or schooling, your riding technique should not differ. This prevents your horse becoming confused, or feeling that he is put under pressure to do something different because it is a dressage test.

Tack

A snaffle bit is all that's required. Under British Dressage rules, from Elementary level and above you can ride with a double bridle if you wish. Refer to the *current* rule book of your national organizing body to check what types of bit and other tack, such as noseband, are allowed in competition. (There are different rules that apply for Quadrille competitions – see Chapter 8.)

A general-purpose saddle will do in the beginning, but if you are going to compete seriously then you may wish to buy a dressage saddle. This just makes it a bit easier so sit in a correct position in the saddle, with your legs placed against the horse's sides under your body. A forward-cut general-purpose saddle will place your thighs in front of your body, which has advantages in other situations, but when riding dressage, a leg position that is more 'straight down' gives you the feeling of being more upright in the saddle. (This, however, is no excuse for collapsing at the waist if you are riding in a general-purpose saddle.)

Rider's Position and Aids

Your riding ability will affect entirely how your horse moves and accepts your aids. First of all, make sure that your position in the saddle is spot on. To do this, you need to sit up tall in the saddle, with your pelvis upright. Lift your chest, and keep your elbows back by your sides. Your hands should be placed equally either side of the horse's withers, with your thumbs uppermost. Maintain a steady contact with the bit: you need to be able to keep the bit still and level in your horse's mouth without pulling. Your elbows, wrists and fingers should support the bit, and at the same time you must be able to feel what is going on in your horse's mouth. This 'feel' indicates to you what is going on at the back end. If he is working correctly, with weight distributed between his hind and forelegs, this should result in a comfortable, elastic contact through the reins.

Your legs should be hanging down by your horse's sides, with your knees and toes to the front. Keep your thighs, knees, and tops of your calves close to his body. You do not need to grip, but you need a contact with your legs.

You must ensure that your aids are very clear. Any confusion between you and your horse may result in overshooting your turns, messing up your transitions, and wiggly centre lines, for example. If your position is good, your aids will be much more effective. Asking your horse to circle by keeping your inside leg near the girth to keep him going and to support him, with your outside leg back a bit to help him turn his back end around the circle, and turning your upper body in the direction you wish to go, is far more effective than leaning in around the circles with your horse going around on two legs and with his back end swinging out on every turn!

HALF-HALTS

To achieve balance and 'self-carriage', so that your horse carries himself, with his head and neck correctly placed, you need to use frequent half-halts. To half-halt, close both legs all the way down and sit up, staying firm through your tummy and lower back for a moment, with your chest up and shoulders square. Keep your elbows by your sides, with your hands closed around the reins, without gripping tightly or pulling back. This action of 'bracing' your position has the effect of asking the horse to step under with his hind legs and lift his back. Be careful not to tighten your backside when you do this, as that would dig your seat into his back, causing him to resist against you and feel lazy. As you 'brace', using all your aids at once, be ready to soften your arms first (without sticking your elbows out). This action should allow the reins to soften without them going loose. If they go loose, your horse may seize the opportunity to overbend. The idea is to make the rein contact a bit firmer, and then soften it. Imagine that the reins are two long elastic bands that are attached to your elbows! Then soften the tone of your body muscles without collapsing. This releases the half-halt.

It may help to think of the half-halt as a 'stop and go' action. The stop aid is the same as beginning to ask your horse to halt, but as soon as you feel him hesitate, ride forward again. This helps him to push off from his hocks when he goes forward after a half-halt.

TRANSITIONS AND THEIR VALUE

Half-halts are the key to good transitions, which make up a large part of every dressage test, so it will pay you to practise half-halts to prepare for halts and all transitions. Progressive transitions are those that go through the gaits in sequence, e.g. halt to walk to trot; canter to trot to walk. Direct transitions are those that 'miss out' a gait, i.e. halt to trot, walk to canter, canter to walk. Downward transitions should not be an ugly mess of pulling on the reins and shoving your feet forwards, bracing against the stirrups, which would most probably wipe out any marks for 'harmony' that you would have been awarded, but a 'tucking under' of the horse's haunches and a rounding of his back and neck (his spine) as he takes weight on his hind legs. In every transition, halt, and half-halt you should sit up and brace through your stomach and back, and close your legs against your horse's sides to support him – a preparatory half-halt to improve your horse's balance is essential to both upward and downward transitions. This procedure is not only beneficial for the horse in that he is far more likely to remain 'round' if you ride him properly; it will also develop his muscles properly, and improve his way of going over time so that you can progress through the levels of test until, hopefully you reach Advanced level in the future.

It is quite difficult to ride an accurate transition at exactly the correct point. Ideally the transition is made as your outside knee, not the horse's nose, is at the letter. The *aids* need to be applied a little earlier, to ensure that the transition occurs where you want it to. Prepare for each transition with a couple of half-halts to maintain your horse's balance. Over-use of the reins in downward transitions looks harsh, and causes resistance from your horse. In upward transitions, keep yourself in a correct position in the saddle, and ensure that your horse moves willingly forward from your leg aids. Avoid pushing and shoving with your seat, as this will cause him to hollow his back and lose the engagement of his hind legs.

The Scales of Training

The Scales of Training are the criteria which determine whether your horse is working properly, and are the aspects that the judge uses to judge your horse's 'way of going'. There are six Scales of Training, which are:

- Rhythm
- Suppleness
- Contact
- Impulsion
- Straightness
- Collection

RHYTHM

Rhythm means regular steps in the horse's gaits – walk, trot, and canter. The walk is four-beat, the trot two-beat, and the canter three beats with a moment of suspension. The best way to develop a sense of rhythm is to ride to music! Tempo is the speed of the rhythm. For example you could ride a working trot at a fast tempo – this does not make it a medium trot. Conversely, a slow trot is not necessarily collected! You should be able to ride a collected, working, medium and extended trot at the same rhythm and tempo. It is the length of stride that changes. A horse with a good rhythm becomes relaxed. A relaxed horse develops suppleness.

SUPPLENESS

A well-trained horse will be supple in two planes: longitudinal (front to back) and lateral (side to side). A horse who is supple front to back will be able to stretch forwards and down, and work correctly 'through his back', i.e. his back should appear to 'swing' or bounce softly up and down. If the horse is tight through his back muscles, the rider will be jolted about. A big-moving horse who does this to the rider is not supple – he is stiff. A supple horse carries the rider effortlessly, enabling the rider to sit still in the saddle. He should give the appearance that everything is going on underneath him with his pelvis slightly tipped under, so that his hind legs are working under the body (engaged) and not paddling along behind.

A laterally supple horse will be able to bend on circles and turns equally in both directions, be supple in his joints, and respond easily to the rider's aids.

A supple horse accepts the rein contact happily in all respects.

CONTACT

The horse should accept the contact from the rider's reins and work happily to the bit with a relaxed jaw. His poll should be the highest point, and his nose vertical to the ground, or just in front of the vertical. If the horse comes behind the vertical, it is important to assess what is going on at the back end. It is most likely that his hind legs are not underneath his body. Acceptance of the contact comes from the horse being able to work in balance and in a correct outline. My own personal guide for a correct contact is the 'scissor test'. If I am judging dressage, I consider what would happen if I cut the rider's reins. Would the horse stay in balance, or would he fall on his head or run away? The rider should be able to soften the rein contact without the horse losing balance. Working into the contact enables the horse to develop power and strength – impulsion.

IMPULSION

Impulsion is the power of the horse, and not, as commonly misunderstood, an increase in speed. A horse who can move slowly and powerfully into a soft, elastic contact, develops the strength to work in collection and remain straight in his work. He should not be held up with the reins, and it should not look as though the rider is working like the clappers to drive the horse forwards.

Impulsion should develop during the horse's training as he becomes stronger through his back and haunches. Driving the horse too much too soon can lead to stresses and strains of the joints and muscles, and you could find your horse suffers from 'wear and tear' and you end up without a dressage horse at all. A horse working with true impulsion should look as though he is covering the ground easily with loose, big strides, without seeming stressed.

STRAIGHTNESS

Straightness is when the horse's hind feet follow the tracks of his forefeet on both straight lines and circles. Horses can find it easier to bend in one direction than the other, and become *more* crooked if this is not corrected. A straight horse works evenly on both sides of his body, and takes weight evenly on both hind legs, the latter being the main criterion for collection.

The rider should easily be able to 'position' the horse for a right or left bend, flexing him at the poll slightly in the direction of the required bend, and bending him in the ribs. Straightness goes hand in hand with suppleness. A supple horse is easy to keep straight. A stiff horse will find ways of evading straightness, usually by swinging his haunches to one side or by tipping his nose rather than flexing properly.

COLLECTION

Collection arises from the ability of the horse to take weight behind, lightening his forehand. Collection develops in degrees according to the standard the horse has reached. The early stage of collection is balance, whereby the novice horse is able to carry the rider without leaning on the reins. To work in balance, his hind legs should be under his pelvis, where they take sufficient weight to prevent the horse going along on his forehand. The advanced horse working in collection can lift his forehand sufficiently to give the impression that he is working 'uphill'. He needs to be able to tuck his pelvis under to a greater degree than a novice horse, requiring more flexion of his hind leg joints. Lightening the forehand enables the horse to perform advanced movements such as canter pirouettes, piaffe and passage. The rider should aim for a light contact with the reins to allow the horse to truly 'work through his back'. Only from correct collection can a horse perform an 'uphill' extended trot, with fore and hind legs working with even steps.

WORKING THROUGH THE BACK

This phrase will occur time after time on your test sheet. You will be marked highly if your horse does 'work through his back', and penalized if he does not. Paying attention to the correct development of the Scales of Training and thus riding your horse in a *correctly* rounded outline will help your horse to 'work through his back' and encourage him to accept a soft and steady contact with the bit. Ideally, your horse takes an even amount of weight on his hind and forelegs; then he is described as balanced.

A horse will achieve a round outline if he is working properly and he should look like a humped-back bridge from his ears to his tail. He should be comfortable to sit on and not jar your back. He should be quietly chewing the bit, not pulling your arms out or conversely tucking his nose behind the vertical and avoiding the contact altogether.

The way to ask a horse to 'work through his back' is to learn to sit properly in the saddle and to half-halt and make transitions correctly.

How to Ride Test Movements Correctly

THE ENTRY

The sign for you to begin, will be either a toot on the horn (if the judge is in a car), or a ringing bell (if the judge is in a gallery or judge's box). At this signal, try not to jump out of your skin, but continue calmly until you reach A for your entry down the centre line. Remember that you have 45 seconds to begin your test after the signal, so don't rush. Make sure you ride an accurate turn down the centre line, and ride straight towards the judge. Try to look business-like, but don't glare at the judge. It helps if you remember to smile, as you will appear more confident.

A straight entry will get you off to a good start, and set you up for the turn away from the centre line at C. Make sure you turn the right way. It is very easy to go wrong at this point. If you do go wrong, you will end up riding your test 'mirror image,' but no one will be any the wiser if you keep your cool, and ride your test as though nothing has gone wrong! This is the beauty of a Freestyle – you can ad-lib where necessary.

CORNERS

The judge will watch how you execute your turn away from the centre line, and how you use the corners. The straightest centre lines can be marred by cutting the turns onto and away from them. Turns and corners should be balanced, and your horse shouldn't change the rhythm of his stride. Allow about six steps to get around a corner. This ensures an even, smooth turn.

CIRCLES

When riding a circle anywhere in the arena, ensure that your circle is round. When circling in the middle of a short side, ride correctly through the first corner of the short side. Do not ride into the second corner, but curve away from the track at either A or C, as appropriate, returning to the same spot to complete your circle. Make sure there is clear distinction between your circles and your corners. When riding a movement at a specific point, aim to execute it as your outside knee is in line with the intended letter.

CHANGES OF REIN

If you intend to change the rein across a long or short diagonal, ride an accurate turn onto the diagonal, leaving the track as your outside knee passes your chosen marker letter. Head off in a straight line, aiming at the far marker letter, giving yourself time to make a second smooth turn onto the track at the end of the diagonal. If you intend to ride medium trot try not to run out of steam too early, as this looks as though you have given up halfway across.

If you intend to ride a 10 m half-circle from the long side and return to the track at a given letter, prepare for the half-circle in good time, making sure that your horse is flexed in the correct direction, and that you are in the correct position. This ensures that you avoid pulling him around at the last moment, which would unbalance him and spoil his rhythm. Make sure that your half-circle touches the centre line, then straighten and ride directly towards the intended letter. As you complete the movement, turn smoothly onto the track, and continue up the long side. (This movement is also known as a demi-volte.)

STRAIGHT LINES

When you ride straight lines, especially up the long sides of the arena, or up the centre line, the judge will look for straightness. Your horse should not be looking to the outside, gazing wistfully at other horses grazing in the next field. Up the long sides, it is expedient to maintain a *slight* flexion to the inside, so that you are always prepared for the next circle or turn. This also helps to focus your horse on the job in hand. Try not to wobble along the boards. These are often set out with large gaps in between, so your horse will tend to waver if he is not secure in his balance.

SERPENTINES

These should be ridden so that they touch each side of the arena. The loops should be even in roundness and size, and make sure that, between the loops, you ride straight across the centre line remaining parallel to the short side. The judge will look for smooth changes of direction and bend. Another version of the serpentine which can be used in Freestyle tests is the loopy version, where you do not straighten as you cross the centre line, but ride directly from loop to loop, with just one or two straight steps as you change direction. This looks good from an artistic point of view and gives you the option of putting in as many loops as you like, but if you overdo it the judge may think you have run out of any other ideas!

LATERAL WORK

Make sure your lateral work is recognizable! The marks are given as a first impression, and an overall impression, for each movement, so riding a sort of leg-yield across the diagonal which undergoes metamorphosis into a half-pass will certainly muddy the marking! You need to make a clear definition where one movement finishes and the next begins.

EXECUTION OF TRANSITIONS

Transitions between one gait and another should be smooth and balanced. You should not need to resort to an emergency pull on the reins in downward transitions, nor overshoot your intended marker. (This is the beauty of Freestyle – no one knows where you are going to do your transitions except you, but you may be caught out by the music unless you have learnt it thoroughly!)

Preparation for each transition with half-halts is essential if you want to give a good impression. Poor transitions will upset your horse and make him tense, which will make him reluctant to 'work through his back'. His back should bounce softly (remain supple) through each transition, and he should appear to step effortlessly from one gait to another without losing his balance.

Amadeus and me at full throttle in extended trot to a powerful piece of music, doing our best to impress the judge.

COLLECTED, MEDIUM AND EXTENDED GAITS

Transitions within the gaits should be clear. The judge has to be able to distinguish between your working and medium canter, for example. I have seen riders who are a bit afraid to 'go for it' in a medium canter, worried that they will not be able to stop the horse at the end of the diagonal. The judge will not be sure that this was intended to be your medium canter until having seen your working canter. This gets even more confusing if you omit your working canter by mistake. Hopefully there will be a bit of a difference between the two otherwise you may get 'no medium canter shown' on your sheet, and a big fat zero as a mark!

FINAL HALT

Make a good turn up the centre line, and prepare for your final halt by collecting your horse with a couple of half-halts. Sit as straight in the saddle as you can, and you should get a square halt. Try not to slow down on your way to the halt, as this will result in a wiggly line and a crooked halt. You need to end as positively as you started. Many a competition has been won or lost on the quality of the halts, so they are worth practising.

In a Freestyle test, the halts have to be clear, so the judge can time your test from the first halt to the last, so try not to fidget around. If your halt is still, but not with your horse standing squarely, at least it is recognizable as a halt. If you fuss too much about trying to make your horse straighten up, you risk him becoming even more lopsided, or even poking his nose in the air, so it is best to leave well alone, and try next time, using your preparatory half-halts more efficiently! Smiling at the judge can help to disperse your nerves, and give you an air that you might know what you are doing, and feel confident about the whole thing. Hopefully the judge will smile back to put you at your ease!

The Test Sheet

MARKS FOR TECHNICAL EXECUTION

In the technical marks section, each movement is marked out of 10, 5 being 'sufficient' and 0 being 'not performed'. Marks of 6 and 7 are very respectable; 8 and 9 very good, and I have not yet met anyone who has scored 10!

Some movements have a coefficient, i.e. they are multiplied by 2 to emphasize the importance of riding them correctly. Checking this on the test sheet before you plan your test can help you to make the most of these marks, by concentrating on the movements with the highest coefficient. For example, if your horse has a talent for half-pirouettes in canter, and they earn double marks in the test you have chosen, take advantage and ensure that they are as good as you can do.

ARTISTIC MARKS

In Freestyle to Music tests, the collective marks are for:

* Rhythm, energy and elasticity.
* Harmony between rider and horse.
* Choreography, use of arena, inventiveness.
* Music and interpretation of the music.
* Degree of Difficulty. Well-calculated risks (from Medium level
  and above).

These marks are multiplied by a coefficient, which varies at different levels to give the total artistic marks. Comments will be given by the judge for both sections where appropriate to help you with your next competition attempt.

WHAT THE JUDGE LOOKS FOR

A dressage judge's comments on your test sheet should generally be encouraging in tone. Judges are aware that every competitor is trying their very best on the day, regardless of the outcome.

Rhythm, energy and elasticity

The judge will take into account the quality and rhythm of all three gaits in this section. Cadence comes across as 'springiness'. A supple horse will be able to produce elasticity in his movement. If he is supple he will be able to 'work through his back' into a soft, steady contact, with his hind legs engaged (under his body). Remember that energy, or impulsion, is not speed but power.

Harmony between rider and horse

The horse should be paying attention to the rider, and not spooking at the geraniums. Horse and rider should appear confident (smiling helps) and the rider should be sitting in a good position, and giving correct aids. This should result in a horse who accepts the contact easily, shows a lightness of his forehand and works in balance.

Choreography, use of arena, inventiveness

The music should be suitable for the horse and the choreography neither too difficult nor too easy. However, it is better to perform a simple routine well than mess up a complicated one. You should ride one of each compulsory movement, but have a contingency plan in case you need to repeat something that does not go quite to your intended plan.

Additional fancy bits can earn higher artistic marks, but a test that is too 'busy' can make the performance confusing and difficult to interpret. Judges like to anticipate what is coming next, otherwise they can become stressed! Unexpected surprises can work – as long as they are not too unexpected and seem completely out of context.

Turnout does not count towards marks, but it does give a workmanlike appearance, and helps convey the impression that you may know what you are doing.

Music and interpretation of the music

You will be judged on the suitability of music to the horse and the interpretation of the music, i.e. astute use of musical phrases, such as fitting medium trot to loud bits, walk to quiet bits, and so on.

Degree of difficulty, well-calculated risks (Medium level and above)

A well-calculated risk means trying something difficult which may or not come off – if it does not, have a fall-back plan so at least the compulsory movements are completed. A wise move is to do the compulsory movements first, leaving a bit of music to play with. Then, if you need to repeat compulsory moves which did not work, you can do so, otherwise you can use some fancy footwork to hopefully increase your score.

Afterwards

However the marks turn out on your sheet, try to analyse your riding for yourself. You will know which parts of your test were good or bad; try to remember which areas you could improve upon. The judge has to comment on your performance in the arena, and we all have good and bad days. Consider dressage tests and riding to music as part of your horse's training, and an indicator of improvements in your riding ability. In this way, competing will be a means to an end, not a stressful experience.

6

YOUR FIRST COMPETITION

A lot of hard work and practice goes into competing, so do make sure you enjoy the actual event. I do think horses and riders generally perform better to music than in conventional tests and this type of competition is becoming more and more popular, and is very attractive to spectators.

Learning the Test

Practising your routine is very important, but above all, learn the music. Play it in the car at every opportunity until you are going through it in your head continually, almost to the point of never wanting to hear it again. This is why it is important to choose music that you really like – otherwise it will drive you mad! By learning the music, you will know where you should be in the arena at any given time so, if you do lose your way, you can catch up without it being obvious. Learn the end of the music coming into the final salute – once you hear this, make a bee-line for X. There is nothing worse than having to make a mad final dash, or getting there too early and having to stand around at a loose end!

Everyone has their own way of memorizing a dressage test. In many conventional dressage competitions it is possible to have your test read out loud for you, but it is advisable to learn it anyway in case your caller has an off-day. In Freestyle tests, this is not possible, mainly because no one except you knows what your next move is – especially if you change tactics mid-test and include a bit of improvisation!

Doodling the patterns on a piece of paper in time with the music saves the embarrassment of being spotted by the neighbours as you run in circles around your back garden! Practise the whole test several times on your horse, so you both know how it fits together, and then practise it in sections without the music to improve your execution of the movements.

When practising the test, if you do not have access at home to an arena of correct dimensions, mark one out with suitable objects in your field or school. Do check that it is the correct size so that you get used to working within its confines. A 20x40 m arena can seem awfully small at first, and the corners tight. A proper dressage arena is usually marked out with white boards (even indoors, where space permits), so practise riding alongside poles, for example, as you will not have the security of a fence to keep you in the arena.

Some tests require a 20x60 m arena. It can seem a very long way across the diagonal in an arena this size, so be sure you can ride a straight line right across from quarter marker to quarter marker.

In addition to practising the test, is also important to practise a warm-up routine at home, which contains all the movements required in your test. Remember that you and your horse need to be warmed up, not worn out! Establish a simple routine encompassing the requirements of the test, but concentrating on loosening your horse up rather than tiring him out. You need enough energy left between you to ride a good test. Stretching exercises to make him supple and frequent transitions to improve his balance are important.

Finding a Competition Venue

There are many ways of doing this. Affiliated competitions, especially those at the higher levels, are usually planned some time in advance and details should be available from your national organizing body. Riding Clubs often put on events (again, these are often planned on an annual basis, and some clubs issue omnibus schedules for the year ahead), some breed societies organize their own shows and many competitions of various levels are advertised in equestrian magazines. Alternatively, you could make inquiries at neighbouring riding stables or livery yards for local venues.

Amadeus as a four-year-old competing at Hickstead. This photo shows harmony, energy and attentiveness – you could not expect more from a young horse. If I remember correctly, we won this class, a Novice Freestyle.

Turnout and Tack

TURNOUT

You and your horse should be neatly turned out. You will need a shirt, tie or stock, jacket (black or navy blue), beige or white breeches, gloves, hat and riding boots. Polish your boots and take an emergency cloth to buff them up before you mount. Long hair should be neatly tied, or in a hair net. A clean, white saddle cloth looks very smart. Although you do not get marks for turnout, it helps to make a good impression and look as though you have made an effort. Dress smartly and try to remain as clean and tidy as you can. This can be difficult if you have a horse who tends to dribble down your gleaming white breeches at the last minute! Amadeus is always doing this to me. He always manages to pinch a last mouthful of hay as I put on his bridle. I have given up trying to wear white gloves, which always get dirty very quickly as I try to deflect the slobber, and have opted for practical black ones!

Plait your horse's mane if you wish (this is almost standard practice, although not compulsory – at least under British Dressage rules) and remember to brush his tail. I have seen competitors who have been in a panic when getting ready – the front end of the horse looks pristine, but they have forgotten the back end, leaving tell-tale strands or straw in the tail or, on one occasion, leaving the tail bandage on, which proceeded to unravel as they entered the arena. Fortunately, this was retrieved by a concerned parent.

TACK

As stated earlier, you do not need a dressage saddle when starting out, but if you are going to compete seriously, it may be worth considering buying one. A well-fitting saddle that is comfortable for both you and your horse is important, as saddle problems can dramatically affect your horse's way of going.

In Freestyle tests under British Dressage rules, snaffle bridles can be used up to and including Advanced level. (Riders in other countries should check their national body's rules.) A snaffle bridle should be accompanied by a cavesson, drop or Flash noseband. In the UK, double bridles can be used at Elementary level and above, but ensure that you can ride your horse correctly in a snaffle bridle before progressing to a double. You are permitted to carry a whip unless the rules state otherwise. Spurs are allowed, but make sure you are competent enough in your riding ability to use them correctly if you need them. You should warm up in the tack that you are competing in.

Note that British Dressage, and other national bodies, have numerous rules relating to details of dress code and equipment. These should be checked in the relevant *current* rule book to avoid inadvertent contravention.

The Test Arena

As stated earlier (Learning the Test) it is important to practise the test in an arena of correct dimensions, but one factor you may not be able to replicate at home is the competition arena surface. Some competition surfaces will be exemplary, others less so.

Arenas on grass are not necessarily mown, or level. Some kind show organizers mow a strip up the centre line, which is extremely helpful. Arenas can be boggy, or have puddles, so it helps if your horse is used to working in adverse conditions. Horses refusing to go through water in the middle of a movement mar many a good test. (Using appropriate studs can help your horse if the ground is slippery – these are permitted under British Dressage rules, but rules of other national bodies should be checked.)

The competition may be held indoors, which can be disconcerting for your horse if he has not been inside a riding hall before. Mirrors can cause spooking or, if your horse is vain, he may stop for a quick look at himself on the way around! At one Christmas Novice competition the organizers had put a beautifully bedecked Christmas tree in one of the corners, so that competitors were changing the rein across the diagonal directly towards the tree. There was quite a bit of back-pedalling in the trot from the horses, and some very panicky expressions on the riders' faces.

Attitude and Preparation

Mention of these issues that may give horses and riders cause for concern brings us to the question of attitude. Being calm and confident is the hardest part of competing. Most people ride very well when warming up but as soon as the starting bell goes they become rigid with fear. (It is very common to worry that everyone else is looking at you, but this is actually not the case. Other competitors are too busy concentrating on their own horses to watch what you are doing.)

When your palms are sweating, your heart pounding, and your shoulders start tensing up, remember that everyone else is probably feeling the same. Unless you can control your reactions, they will result in your horse tensing up, and a hurried test, as you want to get it over with as soon as possible! Try to remember to breathe slowly and deeply. If you make a hash of one element of the test, try to put it out of your mind and concentrate on riding the next movement better.

An extension of this idea is that it is very common to 'lose it' at the end of a good dressage test (as it is to knock down the last fence of a showjumping round). This is usually a consequence of the excitement caused by thinking that you might actually come somewhere – only to do something silly at the end. The way out of this is to treat each competition as training for you and your horse, so you don't wind yourself up into a frenzy trying to win!

OVERCOMING COMPETITION NERVES

Competition nerves can completely wreck a potentially good performance. Keeping them under control is quite an art unless you are lucky enough to be totally laid-back. Superstitions can help – such as wearing your lucky socks, and always putting your left boot on first! However, on a more practical note, there are various things you can do in the lead-up to a competition that will promote a positive attitude and make it less likely that nerve-jangling scenarios will emerge.

Know your horse

The best way to remain confident and to deal with riding nerves in general is to know your horse thoroughly. Understand his capabilities and limitations. You need to know each other very well in order to cope with any strange situations that could make you (or your horse) nervous. If he is afraid, it is up to you to remain calm and confident. Visualize good things happening, not bad. If two motorbikes come tearing up the road while you are out hacking, visualize them as being a long way away from you. This can give you enough thinking time to signal them to slow down, stay tall and calm in a good position in the saddle, and continue riding your horse calmly forward along the road. The bikes will slow down, and you will pass safely. If, on the other hand, you visualize two wild-eyed troublemakers heading directly at you at ninety miles an hour, both you and your horse will end up leaping off the road, with you crouching like a monkey and your horse in a blind panic!

Think positively

The constructive visualization just mentioned works in all sorts of situations, so always try to think positively: turn any 'what-ifs' round on themselves. If you wake up in the night before a competition in a 'state', rather than worrying about what might go wrong, run through your test, visualizing yourself and your horse giving the most perfect performance. Hopefully, this will stay with you in the morning! 'Talking yourself' through a competition in your mind can help your concentration: don't allow yourself any negative thoughts at all.

Be organized

1. Make a list. There's nothing worse than trying to collect all your gear together before you leave for a competition, and frantically trying to

locate missing gloves/car keys/directions, etc. I once had to make three trips back home from the yard for various items, and was consequently late arriving at the competition. Now I have a checklist to follow.

2. Make sure you have reliable transport to get you to the competition in good time. Allow time for tacking up and changing into your show gear (overalls are very useful cover-ups in the interim).

Switch off

Then, to avoid messing up a day completely, it is important to develop a mental 'switch' to shut off the nerves, and get on with the job. Getting stressed with your partner/ mother/ family dog may help at the time but it is not a good idea if you want their help and support next time. Take a deep breath and switch to 'competition mode'. It helps to explain to people that you are not being unfriendly, but focusing. Well, top athletes 'focus' before a competition, so why shouldn't you?

At the Show

Having arrived at the venue in good time and in a settled state of mind, you can improve matters further by attending to your creature comforts. A trip to the loo, a cup of tea and an energy-giving bacon sandwich can be recommended! Make sure you know where you are warming up and which arena you are in. Declare yourself to the steward (if there is one) so that they know you have turned up.

You also need to get your music organized. (As mentioned earlier, it is a good idea to take your music in at least two formats, or to check in advance whether the organizers have any preferences for CDs, tapes or mini discs.) Take your music to the organizers before you warm up, so they can get it to the 'DJ'. Make sure it is clearly labelled with your name, that of your horse, and your class number. The music also needs to be ready to start at the right place, and to have a note on it as to whether the start is at the halt, or at the position outside the arena where you will give a signal.

WARMING UP

It is important to warm up without being fazed by other horses and riders charging around the place. It can be quite daunting coping with a busy arena, and you may find that you have to play 'dodgems' sometimes. Most riders, though, are considerate and stick to the school rules, such as always passing left hand to left hand with an oncoming rider, and not poking each other with whips as they pass. If you are worried about this, it may be worth practising riding with a friend or two on their horses in the school with you before you embark on a competition.

About half an hour should be sufficient time to work in – though this does depend on the temperament of your horse. A nervous horse may need longer to settle down, and need some time in walk just to relax. A lazy horse may need a quick, snappy warm-up, with plenty of transitions to jazz him up. Ride through your pre-planned movements. Personally, I try to ride 10 m circles in each gait on both reins. Then I know my horse is supple and relaxed. Once the competitor before you has entered the arena, you have 5 minutes to get into 'competition mode'. Your horse should be reacting well to your aids. Jazz up your walk, trot and canter so you can go into the arena and show off. Try to get in the mood for your chosen musical theme. This takes a bit of bravado, and confidence, and acting the part. Amadeus and I love our 'ballroom music', which we use for the Prix St Georges test. I use a mental trick of imagining we are dancing around a ballroom dressed to the nines, twirling around to a band. He picks up the mood from me, and definitely shows off!

RIDING THE TEST

Having warmed up, ride over to the competition arena and wait to be called by the steward. Some competitions are 'self-stewarding', in which case you have to check a list in the collecting ring for your start time and be ready to enter the competition area at your allotted time. Also, ask other competitors or bystanders whether the competition is running on time. If it is running late, then you have more time to warm up, but make sure that you do not tire out yourself or your horse. If the competition is running early, you do not have to panic and go before your allotted time if you do not wish to do so (you can if it suits you, and the organizers may thank you for it, but it's your choice). One other point about timing is that, while it is usual (and may be a requirement under the rules) to phone for your dressage times a couple of days in advance, there may be a last-minute change. I have been to several competitions where, on checking with the secretary, I discovered my time to be slightly different from that previously given over the phone. Therefore, it makes sense to check this when you first arrive at the venue.

When it is your turn to compete, make your way to the arena perimeter, and ride around the outside of the white boards. There will usually be room to do this, but if not (as in a small indoor arena), ride around the outside track. The judge may be still marking the sheet of the previous competitor, but will be aware of your presence. Ride around the arena in a purposeful working trot and establish a rhythm. If you can, ride in each direction so your horse has a good look at the arena. Don't be afraid to ride some transitions if you need to. Ensure that your horse is listening and not gazing into the distance. However, do not start using the arena or its environs as a 'warm-up', riding serpentines and suchlike – at this stage you are supposed to remain on the perimeter.

A ringing bell or tooting car horn will signal that the judge is ready for you to start. You then have 45 seconds to get to your starting position. Once you are in position, raise one hand high in the air to signal for your music to start. Take a deep breath, and off you go!

UNDERSTANDING THE SCORE SHEET

Depending on how you think your performance went, you may be either thrilled or dismayed by the time you leave the arena. Personally, I think riding dressage to music is great fun, and I usually enjoy riding a test, whatever the outcome. Competitors are always happy with a good score but it is all too easy to fall into the trap of blaming the judge if you have low marks. As long as your score reflects how your performance went, you should take on board the comments to help you do better next time. Be realistic about your test, and you will find that the judge's comments do make sense. Music is a matter of personal taste, but the judge will be looking to see whether your movements are performed correctly and that your music suits your horse, and should not be influenced by the fact that he or she cannot stand your choice of rock and roll! It is very tempting to go grumbling back to the horsebox if you did not agree with the scores, but if you treat the occasion as part of your horse's training and enjoy the experience of riding your horse to music you will be much more likely to go home in a good mood!

What follows is an explanation of the criteria under which dressage to music is judged.

Technical execution

You will be marked out of 10 for each of the compulsory movements. On the score sheet there are two boxes for each movement, one for the judge's first impression, and one for the final mark. For example, you may do a very good 10 m circle in trot on one rein, and be awarded an 8, and a not so good one to the right, so your final mark for this movement will reflect this, and perhaps drop to a 6. If you ride a poor simple change in one direction, you may get a 5, but you could increase your final mark to a 6 or 7 of you pull off a good one in the other direction.

You will then be given a final mark for Technical Execution. This is added to the total marks for Artistic Impression.

Artistic impression

This covers rhythm, energy and elasticity, harmony between rider and horse, choreography, inventiveness and use of the arena, and interpretation of the music. The mark out of 10 for each of these is multiplied by a coefficient, which can vary from test to test (so do check the test sheet) to give the final total for Artistic Impression.

If the marks for Technical Execution are out of 120, and the artistic marks are also out of 120, your total marks will be out of 240, and worked out as a percentage score. For example, if your average scores for the movements are close to 6, you should end up with a score of around 60%.

The boxes beside the marks are for the judge's comments, such as 'Imaginative choreography', or 'Lacking suppleness', for example. 'Test too busy for the horse today' and 'Could add more variation' are also valid comments you may come across.

Whatever your score, you will hopefully have enjoyed the experience, and will want to have another go in the near future. You can use the same test and music as many times as you want – until you become bored with it and fancy a change! It helps to ride the same routine in competition several times, adjusting it here or there as necessary to improve your marks.

7

QUADRILLE RIDING

uadrille riding is where a group of riders, essentially four, but sometimes larger groups, ride in formation.

Performing in a group accustoms horses to working in close proximity to each other and is good preparation for coping with a busy warm-up arena at a show. Besides which, riding in a Quadrille is very good discipline for every horse and rider, and I think everyone should have a go at it at some point during their riding career.

A Pas de Deux is ridden by two riders and is a good precursor to riding in a larger group. Getting your horse used to working alongside another is useful when hacking for example, as is riding in front of or behind another horse. A Pas de Deux can be made up of movements ridden side by side, or one behind the other, or mirror images. A combination of all three works well in a routine.

My own first experience of Quadrille riding to music was in Germany. The riding centre held a Quadrille session every week, on a Friday evening, which I ended up commanding. I would stand in the corner on a box and yell at the top of my voice, in German. (German is a very good language for bellowing, as the words are quite hard sounding, which gives you an air of authority!) On festivals, especially at Christmas, everyone would dress up according to which *Fest* it was. There were a lot of calls for *'Eine runde schnapps'* to be brought into the arena for the participants, especially if anyone parted company from their horse. This became

more likely as more schnapps was consumed! The costumes were fairly
elaborate, as many clients kept their own outfit for yearly use, and added to
it on a regular basis.

Influences of Major Schools on the Quadrille

Down the centuries, the work of major schools of equitation has had
a great influence on the development of Quadrille riding.

THE SPANISH RIDING SCHOOL OF VIENNA

The Spanish Riding School in Vienna is the only riding academy in the
world which has been cultivating the art of classical equitation for over 400
years and which trains both horses and riders according to methods which
have been used for centuries – most of them passed down through word
of mouth. The Imperial Riding School was originally founded in 1572,
adjacent to the Imperial Palace (the Winter Riding Hall, still famous
worldwide today, was built in 1735), being built for the teaching and
practice of the young nobility and also for the training of the horse in the
art of riding and in battle.

During that era, equestrian ballets and riding carousels were very
popular. They were an opportunity for the Emperor to show off his
prowess as a horseman, and the skills of his army. Riding in formation was
part of every soldier's training, so the ranks could be kept close together.
The following is an example of a major event based on a description in
Hans Handler's book *The Spanish Riding School.*

Emperor Leopold I was a music lover and celebrated his wedding
to Margareta Theresa with a magnificent event. The ballet took place
in the inner courtyard of the Imperial Palace in Vienna, with a centre-
piece of a large wooden ship, complete with billowing sails. The event
began with the Emperor heading a procession, in which about 300
people took part, including many members of the nobility all dressed
in elaborate robes, carried by a huge float which was drawn by eight
white horses. Knights portrayed the four elements of Fire, Earth, Water
and Air, performing elaborate moves around the Emperor, including
High School movements, or 'airs above the ground', such as the
courbette, in which the horse rears up on his hind legs, and jumps
forwards.

The ballet itself was composed of several 'acts' or performances:

1. High School movements were performed by the Emperor and four other riders.
2. Four more horses and riders joined the display.
3. The four knights portraying the four elements entered the display at a gallop, and rode different patterns around the Emperor, such as serpentines and circles. Each pattern was repeated 'mirror image' so that the spectators surrounding the courtyard could appreciate their riding skills.
4. The Emperor, accompanied by another group of eight riders, performed further airs above the ground accompanied by music.
5. The next set of movements included more intricately woven patterns, including small circles (voltes) and yet more courbettes.
6. Six horses, who where known as 'jumpers', performed 'airs above the ground' such as the capriole, in which the horse jumps up, then kicks out with his hind legs. The Emperor and the eight riders with him performed courbettes again.
7. Twelve riders moved into two semi-circles around the Emperor.
8. A mock capture of the Emperor ensued, from which he 'escaped' before being 'recaptured.'

The horses were given a breather in walk, accompanied by music played by a large number of violins, to which they marched in time.

9. The ballet continued, with crossed diagonal patterns and small circles. The horses then formed a double cross with the Emperor in the centre, performing yet more courbettes.
10. The riders portraying the Four Elements performed a new pattern.
11. Four more riders rode to the bride's box and performed caprioles, directly underneath the box.

Then, in the courtyard, three concentric circles were formed, which rotated like a wheel.

12. The finale was the well-organized exit of all the participants in the tableau.

During this display, footmen and pages had moved into position around the courtyard. Over 1,300 people took part overall, and this was probably the first time the Lipizzaner horses had performed to music.

Today, the performance of the Spanish Riding School is legendary, and is a must for all horse enthusiasts, especially if you can go to see them in Vienna at the Winter Riding School. Their performance to classical music is usually as follows:

1. **Quadrille** of eight young stallions, showing accuracy of the movements and the concentration required between horse and rider.

2. **Movements of the Classical School** are shown by four riders and their horses

3. **Pas de Deux**, in which two riders work together and in mirror image in symmetrical patterns.

4. **In-hand work**, when piaffe is shown by one horse between the pillars in the centre of the arena, and others show piaffe and passage, and the 'airs above the ground' such as the levade, courbette and capriole. The horses are worked from the ground by their riders.

5. **Work on long-reins**, when a single horse is worked from the ground by his rider who guides him through different movements from behind the horse. The horse has to be highly trained in order to be sensitive to the rider's imperceptible aids.

6. **The airs above the ground** are ridden under saddle. This display is made even more impressive because the riders ride without stirrups. How they stay on is unbelievable, but I expect the chamois leather breeches help!

7. **The School Quadrille** echoes the horse ballets of the past and it is a highly co-ordinated display of precision. It always brings tears to my eyes, and I must have seen the performance six times!

A display by the Spanish Riding School.

97

The riders are highly skilled in perfection. Their horses work throughout the movements in exactly the same way, performing all the lateral work with identical angles, keeping pinpoint accurate distances between each horse, and all responding impeccably to the smallest of aids. It *looks* very easy, but it takes years of practice to become that skilled. If you watch very, very closely, you may notice the newer horses making the odd mistake, or becoming a little excited, but these incidents are so well-handled by the riders that you have to quite alert to spot them! The riders introduce a young horse very carefully to these events when they are on tour, in different venues around the world, and you may notice a horse quietly walking and not performing many 'airs above the ground' – just one or two to accustom him to the atmosphere.

Watching the horses being trained during morning exercise in Vienna is very interesting. You will see the riders working alone to perfect movements with their horses, then in small groups to accustom the horses to working in close proximity to each other.

THE FRENCH CAVALRY SCHOOL AT SAUMUR

Following France's defeat in the Seven Years War, King Louis XV of France was keen to produce a powerful, skilled cavalry, and he had several schools built, the most famous being at Saumur, founded in 1763. Saumur became so successful that, by 1771, all the other schools except Lunéville had disappeared. The Royal Cavalry itself changed base several times, including being located at the palace of Versailles before settling at Saumur.

The instructors at the Cavalry School wore blue coats and were known as the Cadre Bleu. The royal instructors were given a black uniform to distinguish them from everyone else, and became known as the Cadre Noir. In 1972, the School became incorporated into the Ecole Nationale d' Equitation, which trains riders in all disciplines, but still preserves the ancient French style of Quadrille, and continues to give outstanding performances in school movements, including the 'airs above the ground'.

THE ROYAL ANDALUSIAN SCHOOL OF EQUESTRIAN ART

The Royal Andalusian School of Equestrian Art is in southern Spain, in Jerez de la Frontera. This area is also renowned for sherry production, so well worth a visit if you like sherry and horses! The school has become famous for its show entitled 'How the Andalusian Horses Dance', which is a unique exhibition of horsemanship. In May 1975 his Majesty King Juan Carlos I – at that time Prince of Spain – awarded Don Alvaro Domecq Romero the Golden Horse trophy in recognition of his work and dedication to the horse. In honour of this award, Alvaro Domecq presented this show for the very first time, which in turn led to the foundation of the school as we know it today.

In 1986 the School acquired the stable of Don Pedro Domecq de la Riva, which consisted of thirty-five Spanish horses and a wonderful collection of horse-drawn carriages, some dating back to 1730, along with saddles and embroidery for both horses and coachmen.

The School trains riders and horses in *Alta Escuela* (classical dressage) and upholds the traditions of breeding the Spanish horse, the traditions and culture which relate to Spanish horsemanship, and acts as an ambassador of Spain on annual tours around the world.

The School's display includes a ride of four stallions showing school movements, in-hand work displaying the airs above the ground, and work on piaffe and passage and Spanish walk. They also show a Quadrille of carriages with different formations of horse such as 'tandem' (with one horse behind the other), a pair (two horses side by side) and a group of five, with three horses in front and two behind.

Another part of the programme has three horses under saddle working mostly side by side or closely one behind the other. They also show the airs

Two riders of the Royal Andalusian School of Equestrian Art in action.

above the ground under saddle. The show ends with a Quadrille of twelve riders showing clever patterns with half the ride splitting off, riding small voltes side by side and effortlessly merging again with the other riders. Another impressive move involves coming down the centre of the school in threes, then filtering off into two separate rides at the end of the centre line, with two riders going one way, and one the other. This alternates with each three riders i.e. two to the right, one to the left, and the next group one to the right and two to the left. I should think this pattern alone takes a great deal of practice and a good memory! The ride also includes interlocking diagonals in half-pass at the canter with two rides of six crossing over between the pillars, which are in the middle of the school either side of the centre point. Although the classical movements are the same as the other great Schools, the atmosphere is quite different and wonderful to witness.

THE PORTUGUESE SCHOOL OF EQUESTRIAN ART

The Portuguese School of Equestrian Art in its current form has evolved from the Portuguese Royal Academy which used horses from the Alter Real Stud, founded in 1748 by King Joao V. Both he and his son, Don Jose I, were keen horsemen and they set up a breeding and training programme for the cavalry at the Royal Manège using the bravest and best-performing horses. King Jose's Master of the Horse was the Marquess of Marialva, who specialized in the work of the High School. His code of rules for classical dressage and mounted bullfighting is still in use today. Although the original School went into decline during the Peninsular Wars and subsequent revolutions, it was revived in the early 1980s, its traditions having been kept alive by the old family breeders of the Lusitano horse. Even today, the teachings of Marialva are passed on from father to son, master to pupil in the time-honoured way.

The stud of royal horses is still in existence at Alter do Chao and the temporary home of the revived Portuguese School of Equestrian Art is the Queluz Palace, just outside Lisbon. The bay stallions perform regularly in the grounds of the palace. Their display, in traditional tack and costume, is similar to the other great Schools, demonstrating work in hand and on long reins, as well as the 'airs above the ground'. They demonstrate a 'Pas de Trois' as well as a finale of up to ten riders in the Quadrille.

The Portuguese School of Equestrian Art in display formation and riding a Pas de Trois.

Performing a Quadrille

WHAT CAN GO WRONG

A Quadrille of professional riders performing in public usually looks so impressive, with not a horse out of line and all the riders appearing to be cool calm, and collected. Apart from those already mentioned, some of the famous musical rides around the world are those of the Household Cavalry, the Metropolitan Police and the Royal Canadian Mounted Police. In Germany, the State studs hold stallion parades regularly, and these include

Quadrille riding, one of the most impressive I have ever seen being in Dillenburg.

However, performing a Quadrille with a number of horses and riders does not necessarily go to plan. Many hours of training can cover most eventualities, but the unexpected can still happen and it best to have a contingency plan. That is why I'm going to talk about some of the things that *can* happen before discussing movements and planning.

When riding in a group, it is most important not to fall off! You will be in close proximity to other horses, and run the risk of being trampled on. Though horses will do their best not to stand on you deliberately, there may not be sufficient room for them to move out of your way, and one may panic. If this does happen, the best thing is to lie still until the other riders and horses are at a safe distance. Hopefully, the other riders will have the presence of mind to ride past you and not over you and come to a halt at a safe distance. Your horse should be caught by a helper (this is very good reason for having a couple of people on standby should accidents happen).

Some horses can become very excitable when ridden in a group the first few times. I have seen a horse 'breaking ranks' at a gallop from a line of sixteen horses abreast, taking the horse either side with him. It took quick reactions from the riders to 'slam on the brakes' and resume their places with the rest of the group, thus avoiding a stampede.

If your horse has a bucking fit, you have two options. Either turn away from the rest of the ride, perform your solo 'bronco' act and return to your place once you have regained decorum or, if you are sandwiched in between two others, remain in place and sit tight until your horse calms down. If the horse either side of you is under control, this is probably the best option, as your horse will calm down more quickly. In these situations you, and your team mates, need nerves of steel, and a secure seat!

It is all too easy to have a 'blank moment' and forget the next movement. You could be distracted by camera flashes going off, sudden noises, loud clapping and so on. If you do go the opposite way to your team mates try not to panic, but make your way calmly back into the formation at the appropriate opportunity. Hopefully the audience will think you are doing your 'solo piece' and will not be aware that your deviation was accidental!

Some horses react to outside influences more than others. It does help if your horse is correctly 'on your aids' so that you can keep his attention, but if your horse does 'go deaf' to your aids, stay calm, and concentrate on keeping your place in the ride. Hopefully the other team members will be calm, and their influence will help him to settle down. It does not help, however, if your team mates become annoyed with you. This will not help you to keep your cool, and it all may end in tears!

If you are riding in costume, it can happen that the 'props' fail to work, in which case, try to get rid of them as soon as possible. I had such an occasion with a parasol which was substituted for my faithful umbrella at the last moment. Having not practised with it very much, I forgot how to put it down, so was stuck with trying to control my horse with one hand when two would have been much better!

It is more important to have a good ride than to worry too much about the 'frills'. If you are unsure about any aspect of your costume, it can be a distraction from the job in hand – which is to ride well. A few years ago I watched a fantastic display of horses 'skipping' in canter over 'skipping hoops' held by their riders. The horses were kept straight with side reins attached to their saddles, while the riders used both arms to 'skip' so their horses jumped through the hoop with each canter stride. This was very impressive, especially when done over small jumps. One horse, however, began to increase his speed. The rider, with a look of panic on his face, turned his 'skipping hoop' faster and faster to keep up with his horse, and very sensibly headed for the exit, where they were grabbed by other team members. What was impressive was the rider's display of horsemanship, and the ability to maintain an impeccable seat in the saddle throughout.

Quadrille riding is all about team work, and helping each other out should a problem arise. It is very important to work this out beforehand if you can, but often you have no idea what could happen, so you will learn from experience. These are just some of the things that can happen but do speak to riders who have ridden in Quadrilles to see if they can give you any further helpful tips. I am sure there are many more stories of 'what went wrong on the day'!

SAMPLE MOVEMENTS

Here are some sample movements for riding in a Quadrille. They are not in any specific order, but are ideas that can be joined together to make a full routine. The first six diagrams show patterns performed by eight riders.

1. Keeping four abreast, ride a series of turns straight across the arena.

2. Commencing on the track in single file, ride across the short diagonals of the arena to form a V shape.

3. Ride down the centre line in single file. Split off at the end of the centre line, alternate riders turning right and left. To remember where you are going, turn the opposite way from the rider in front of you! Keep in line with the rider on the other side of the school.

4. As you reach the short side, turn down the centre line in pairs. At the end of the centre line, turn away in pairs and proceed up the track side by side.

5. Ride down the centre line in fours. At the end of the centre line, turn away in fours side by side.

6. Turn down the centre line to form one line of eight. The two riders starting the turn on the inside will have to do a very small turn, and the ones on the outside a large turn. Proceed down the centre line in your formation. This makes a good finale to a Quadrille, as you are lined up for the final salute.

Alternatively, you can unravel the ride by reversing the above movements. This is a good routine for novice riders (provided that the horses all get on with each other!). It can be performed in walk or trot.

7. This exercise is 'the wheel', a great favourite of Quadrille riders as it looks very dramatic when ridden well. The riders proceed four abreast up the long side. At a suitable point, say halfway along, the ride begins to turn off the track onto a large circle. The inside rider has to keep a steady pace, while the one on the outside has to motor on for everyone to remain level with each other on the circle. You can make as many turns of 'the wheel' as you like before you straighten up and finish by going down the long side, remaining in a line of four.

8. Riding four abreast, ride a 20 m half-circle to the centre line of the school. As you reach the centre line, change direction and ride a half-circle on the other rein.

A selection of Quadrille movements to try.

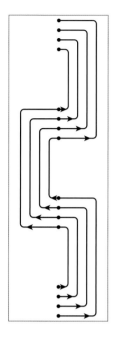

1.

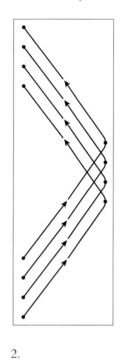

2.

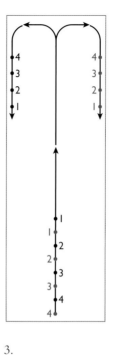

3.

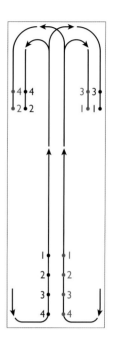

4.

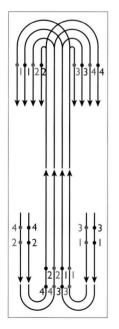

5.

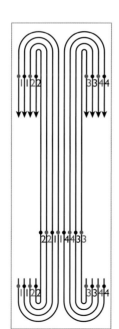

6.

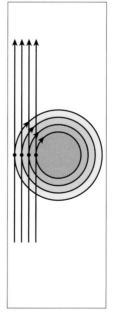

7.

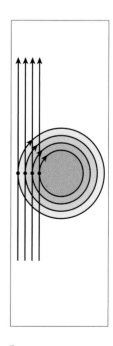

8.

Continued.

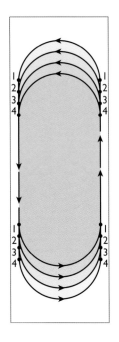

9.

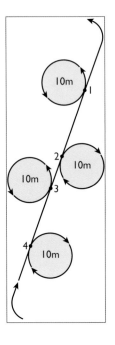

10.

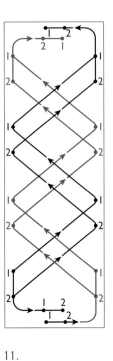

11.

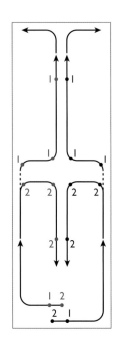

12.

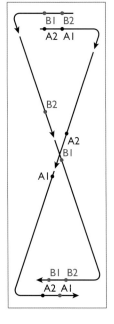

13.

Quadrille riding in Sweden on one of my training courses at the Nobynas Stud. Although this is a Friesian stud, the team consists of other breeds. From the left: Penilla and Bethan with their Icelandic ponies, Eva on her Dales and another Eva on someone else's Arab gelding. Trying to command a Quadrille with an assortment of breeds and two riders named Eva led to much hilarity and some 'interesting' movements.

9. Starting one behind the other on the long side, ride a 20 m half-circle to the other long side, where you should meet the track one behind the other. Continue up the long side and ride another 20 m half-circle to correspond with the first one. You should remain side by side on the half-circles and all cross the centre line at the same time!

10. Change the rein across the long diagonal, keeping well spaced out. The first rider should be the same distance from the far quarter marker as the last rider is from the first quarter marker. Turn alternate 10 m circles going the opposite way to the rider in front of you. You should all finish your circles at the same point you started from. Proceed along the diagonal. This can be repeated on the next diagonal, but the riders will need to circle in the opposite direction from last time so that the first and last riders have room to circle away from the track or wall, otherwise they will not have enough room.

11. Start with two riders on each rein, one behind the other, the pairs passing left hand to left hand on the short side. Ride a series of short diagonals across the school to the other side, each pair remaining side by side as they cross the arena.

12. Start with two riders on each rein, one behind each other on the short side of the arena. Turn up the long sides, one behind the other. Halfway up the school, turn across to the centre line in pairs. You should meet the other pair head on. Turn away from the riders you meet, and you will have a new partner to ride up the centre line with. Turn away from each other as you reach the short side. You are then in a position to repeat the movement as many times as you like. To get out of this pattern, after meeting up on the centre line, you could all turn the same way in pairs instead of going in opposite directions.

13. Start with two riders on each rein, one behind each other on the short side of the arena. Change the rein across the diagonals, passing through the gaps between the horses at X. This can look very dramatic, especially at a canter or extended trot! This can be repeated on the next diagonal, but you will find the lead horse changes each time, so make sure you know whose turn it is to go first.

KEEPING YOUR DISTANCES AND SPACING

If you have horses well-matched in size and length of stride, it makes life fairly easy when it comes to riding a Quadrille. If you are entering a

The victorious Chipstead Riding Club presenting themselves immaculately to a 'full house' at Olympia in readiness for their afternoon performance. The horses are equally spaced, giving a very slick impression.

The Chipstead Riding Club's winning performance at Olympia. A great deal of concentration is required to ride accurately. Co-ordination between riders entails knowing where you should be at any given moment and keeping the same speed and rhythm as your team mates.

high-powered competition, then this does matter, but anyone who is eager to have a go for fun should not be hoofed off the team just because their horse is too big, or too small, fast or slow, or with a long or short stride. A small pony will often be quicker that a big horse with a long stride, so overall everyone has a good a chance of being able to manage fairly well. The only time they could be asked to give it a miss is if the horse or pony is badly mannered or out of control, which could put other horses and riders at risk.

It all comes down to the skill of the rider to keep up or hold back to maintain the desired distance from the horse in front. To start with, it can help to put the more forward-going horse at the front of the ride, and the slowest at the back. You may not know which is which until the riders start to form a ride. You may need to switch places about to get the best combination. It also helps to choose a sensible leading file, who checks on the ride frequently to see if everyone is keeping up. A lead rider who goes careering off at a spanking trot, oblivious of the rest of the ride, will just leave everyone trailing in their wake. Conversely, a leading file who is too slow can be as infuriating as some dawdler driving their car down a country lane at 10 mph – which can lead to frustrated riders and cross horses bunching together.

It is a good idea that as many riders as possible have a go at being leading file, as some movements will require a change of lead horse. Quite often the horse at the rear of the ride has to take the lead if the ride changes direction, for instance when turning across the school. As riders learn to take responsibility for the rest of the group, you should find that they all manage to alter their horse's speed accordingly; the slower ones speed up, while the faster ones slow down. Once this stage is reached, all horses and riders should be able to work in any position in the ride.

It can happen for various reasons that you have a rider missing from a practice session, so you have to leave a gap for them and work with an 'imaginary' horse and rider in the ranks. It helps if the 'virtual rider' is rear file, so the patterns where you are in single file are not affected, but the last 'real' rider will have to work solo.

Warming up for our first-ever attempt at *Mary Poppins*. At this point, we need to even out our spacing. The rider at the back is in the best position to shout commands to the others to make improvements. (That's me!)

Riding in single file

The standard distance you should be from the horse in front of you is one horse's length, but this can be difficult to determine, depending on how big you imagine 'a horse' to be and, perhaps, on how big the horses actually are. Some riders could fit an elephant between their horse and the one in front, and others 'tailgate' the backside of the horse ahead of them. They probably drive their cars in the same way on the motorway! A sensible guideline for one horse's length is to keep back until you can see the hocks of the horse in front of you. To ride half a horse's length apart, which gives a more team-like effect to the ride formation, close up until you can see the top of the horse's tail in front. (There is a bit of leeway here if you have a 12.2 hh pony behind a 17 hh Clydesdale). When riding in single file up the centre line, try to keep in line with the rider in front of you. Stare at the back of their riding hat to help you stay behind them. Both when training and judging I have often had a ride so straggly travelling towards me down the centre line, that I could see every single rider. I just want to see the first rider, and not the others!

Riding in pairs

When you are riding side by side with another rider, try to keep your knee level with theirs. This does not mean playing 'bumper cars' with them and causing bruised kneecaps; close proximity will do. If your horses do not allow you to get this close at first, you have to ride at a safe distance apart

Riding as a pair in a training session. Learning to keep as a pair, and not to drift apart or get one behind the other, takes some practice. When you first start, it is best to keep a little lateral distance while the horses get used to working side by side. One they are settled, you and your partner can move closer.

(half a metre) until they have stopped pulling faces at each other and relaxed. Then you can move closer. It is important to keep your horse straight so his backend does not inadvertently bump against the other horse, which could result in someone getting kicked. Ride correctly with your legs on your horse's sides to help with the steering, and keep an even contact with the reins to keep your horse's neck straight, so that he cannot take a quick bite out of his partner. If your reins are too long, then you risk him misbehaving.

Paired riders should have a chat between themselves about how fast or slow they should be going. Try to find a happy medium so both horses can work comfortably together, and one is not surging ahead while the other is hitting reverse.

Riding in a line of four or more

If you are in a line of four or more, side by side, you need to keep in line with a designated lead rider, who is usually one of the end riders. The way to do this is as follows. Let's say the lead rider is the one on the far right. The rider to the lead rider's left has to look to the right to keep level with the lead rider. All the other riders should look to their right to check that they are level with the rider on their right. The terminology is to 'dress right'. (This has nothing to do with tailoring and inside leg measurements by the way – it actually has the same root as 'dressage'.) Conversely, if your lead rider is to your left, you would 'dress left.'

Corners and turns

When turning, the inside rider has to make a much smaller turn than the one on the outside. The other riders turn somewhere in between. You should all keep 'knee to knee'. Also, the horse on the inside has to be kept collected enough to maintain the walk, trot or canter, if possible. The rider on the outside has to ride more forwards.

'Wheeling'

Riding a wheel formation can look very impressive, especially with eight riders. The rider on the inside has to ride a small circle in a collected walk. The outside rider will probably be cantering, or in an extended trot. The other riders have to gauge their gait with reference to the speed at which the 'wheel' is travelling – which might range from collected trot up to medium trot. If the inner rider cannot keep to a collected walk, the outside rider will be going like the clappers! The riders should keep knee to knee, and the horses should all be flexed correctly in the direction of the circle to avoid face-pulling.

Riding synchronized circles (for example, movement 10 in Sample Movements page 107)

The horses should be spaced further apart than usual when trying this exercise, so that when the first rider is approaching the end of the diagonal, the last rider is on the beginning of the diagonal. The first rider should circle away from the side of the arena; otherwise they will not have enough room to circle. Each rider circles the opposite way from the rider in front, with the last rider also circling away from the outside of the arena. This will work if there is an *even* number of riders in the Quadrille.

Riding changes out of the circle (from one direction to the other)

When changing from one circle to the other, the inside rider will become the outside one, and vice versa, so the riders have to be on the ball, as they will all either be pushing on or holding back as they change direction. As the riders cross the centre line together they should all be travelling at the same speed for a few steps. The new outside rider then forges ahead, and the inside rider collects. As the ride approaches the centre line for a second time after completing one circle, the ride should aim to be side by side and straight, before the inside and outside riders change roles again. The other riders should aim to keep evenly placed between the outer riders.

Riding across the diagonals, crossing at X (see movement 13 in Sample Movements page 107)

This always a 'crowd-pleaser' and just as much fun to ride. Two rides should be formed, one travelling on the right rein, and the other on the left rein. I will call them ride A and ride B, and assume two riders in each. The two rides pass left hand to left hand on the short side, then change the rein across the diagonal. It is safer if the riders keep one and a half horse's lengths apart to avoid collisions during this manoeuvre! The ride on the inside (ride A) will take the lead across the diagonal. The first rider, A1 sallies forth. Rider B1 passes through the gap between riders A1 and A2. Rider B2 crosses the centre point of the diagonal behind rider A2. All riders should keep straight and exactly on their respective diagonal lines.

COVERING UP MISTAKES

These aren't the more bizarre mistakes mentioned earlier in What Can Go Wrong, but rather more run of the mill glitches. If a rider gets left behind, the best place to catch up is on a corner. By cutting the corner slightly, they can make up the gap that has appeared between them and the rider in front. If a rider goes the wrong way, they can keep going at the same gait as the rest of the ride, and quietly slot back in at a suitable place. It is up to the other riders to help this rider out, and leave them a gap to fit into. When working in pairs, if the inside rider does not leave enough room for the rider outside, they should go one behind the other for a few steps, then resume the pair formation. It is up to the inside rider to shove over and let the other rider alongside. If you are the outside rider, and it look as though you are going to be squashed against the wall by your partner, shout! It is very important to communicate to each other. You do not have to hurl abuse, but saying 'speed up a bit', or 'give me more room' should not give offence! Mistakes do happen, and it is important not to blame each other.

ADVICE FOR INSTRUCTORS

Quadrille riding is supposed to be fun as well as a test of horsemanship. The success of a Quadrille is down to the skill of the instructor, and their ability to give clear commands in time for the riders to react accordingly on cue. Late commands result in confusion, such as riders over-shooting the arena letters, or, in the worst scenario, collisions when two rides are working in opposite directions. It can end in tears all too easily when tempers are frayed (the instructor) and the person at the rear of the ride cannot hear the instructions (and goes home early in disgust). Here are my tips for commanding a successful and jolly afternoon's Quadrille riding:

- Choose suitable music that is easy to listen to. Background music can be helpful, such as 'big band' or orchestral music that can be left to play while you drill the ride rather than worrying about choreographing movements exactly to the music – or you could use a selection of familiar pop songs. You do not want to be worrying too much about everyone fitting exactly to the music to start with, but it does help the riders to relax and enjoy themselves if you have a tempo that most horses and ponies can manage.

- Speak loudly and clearly. There is no need to shout, but you do need to project your voice so all the riders can hear you. (If you are lucky enough to have the luxury of a radio-mike you will still have some voice left at the end.) You may need to explain the moves without the music first, so your commands are audible. Or you could just have the music playing quietly.

- When working with riders and horses you are not familiar with, allow them to work for a few minutes in open order in walk and trot (doing their own thing) to give you a chance to assess who would be a likely leading file, and which order to put the horses and riders in. Save the canter work for later, when you have the ride under control! The faster ones should go at the front of the ride, and the slower ones at the back. Otherwise you will end up with riders either 'tailgating' each other or leaving large spaces in between.

- Once you have selected your leading file, ask the riders to form a ride one behind the other, leaving one horse's length between. Instruct the leading file to check behind from time to time to ensure an appropriate speed, so that the others are neither hammering along to keep up, nor going too slowly and causing a pile-up. If the leading file is having problems, let another rider take over. This should be done tactfully, not by relegating the poor rider to the ranks, feeling a total failure before the Quadrille has begun.

- Keep the ride in walk while they familiarize themselves with riding in a group. These days, many riders do not get the chance to ride together, so they have to understand that they must watch out for each other, as well as the instructor casting a beady eye over every rider during the Quadrille. This is not the time to show off as an individual, but to learn to work as a team!

- Rehearse some easy movements in walk, keeping the ride one behind the other (in single file). The command would be, 'Ride, prepare to walk on in single file, ride WALK.'

- Numbering the ride in twos from the beginning is a good idea for later on in the session, when you introduce working in two rides. The first rider calls out 'ONE' in a loud voice over the inside shoulder so the rider behind can hear. The second rider shouts out 'TWO', the third rider 'ONE', and so on. The command is, 'Ride, from the front, number in twos.' They will probably look blankly at you, so you will have to explain what you mean first, as above. They need to remember if they are a ONE or a TWO for the duration of the ride.

- To turn the ride down the centre line, say, 'Ride, prepare to turn down the centre line at A in single file, RIDE TURN.' The riders should be one behind the other. Advise them to line themselves up with the rider's hat in front of them. If you stand at C at this point you should see just the first rider coming towards you, and not the whole ride straddling either side of the centre line.

- At the end of the centre line at C, split the ride into two. Say, 'At C, number ones turn left, and number twos turn right. TURN.' Instruct the riders to keep level with their opposite number on the other side of the school.

- 'Ride turn down the centre line in twos. TURN.' They should turn down the centre line as pairs, as close together as the horses will allow. If you find two horses (or riders!) really do not get along, then change the ride around so they have new partners.

- 'At C, first pair turn left, second pair turn right and so on. TURN.' Make sure the outside rider pushes on a bit, and the inside rider holds back, so the riders stay 'knee to knee' with each other. 'Proceed up the long side in twos.'

- 'At A down the centre in fours. TURN.' Most riders will be able to do this, but you need a good group to go on to the next stage, which is to turn down the centre line as a line of eight, so it is wise to 'unwind' the ride again once you have them four abreast down the centre line. Peel them off in twos, then singly until they are in single file again in their original order.

- Once this is successful in walk, try it in trot to the music. If you need to command the moves again, you will have to be heard over the music; alternatively, have your hand on the volume button, and just turn it down while you speak.

- To work in two rides, split the ride ones to the left, and twos to the right as before, but keep them as two separate rides. 'Rides pass left hand to left hand at A and C' prevents head-on collisions. They should leave a sensible gap between the two rides to avoid a clashing of kneecaps en route. A fun exercise is to change the rein across the diagonals of the school, with the riders passing between each other at X. As an instructor, you have to have your wits about you for this, to keep the riders going through the correct gaps. For a novice group, walk or a slow trot is advisable, but a more experienced group will want to do it at extended trot, or canter! Just make sure you keep control of the lot of them and make sure the rides continue to pass left to left on the short sides.

- To get the riders back into one ride again, you could ask them to come down the centre line, filtering into their original order one behind the other. (Hopefully, they can remember who they were behind at the beginning.)

If you are inexperienced at commanding a ride, stick to simple school movements and make sure they are ridden well. If you make things too complicated you may confuse the riders and they could lose faith in your ability to keep control of the proceedings! It may help to work with a more experienced instructor, who can advise you and take over if necessary. Commanding part of a Quadrille as distinct from the whole session can ease you into it. Confidence is the main criterion, but you need good powers of observation to keep track of all the riders at the same time – and a good sense of humour!

8

QUADRILLE COMPETITIONS

Many Riding Clubs and equestrian organizations have their own Quadrille team and run competitions and displays. In the UK, the British Riding Clubs organization runs a Quadrille competition, with a qualifying round in the autumn, followed by a final at the Olympia Horse Show which is held just before Christmas.

The practical prerequisites for entry to a Quadrille competition are that the horses and riders are competent at Novice level, skilled enough to work as a team, and able put on an exciting display. Simple school movements should be put together in an interesting way to tell a story. The horses and riders do not have to be at Grand Prix level! The team should have a 'name' and their routine should have a theme.

The horses should be immaculately turned out with their manes and tails similarly plaited, dressed with ribbons and so on – though they can be adapted individually if the team has separate characters, such as 'Goldilocks and the Three Bears'.

All the tack should be cleaned to within an inch of its life and must be in good condition and fit properly. The tack for all four horses should match as closely as possible, bearing in mind that it is not practical to buy new saddles and bridles for the occasion! Matching browbands and nosebands can give the impression of unity, as can matching saddle cloths and rubber stirrup treads. The team I ride with has competed with one horse in a double bridle, and the others in snaffles successfully – again, this

Our first-ever attempt at
Merrist Wood College
in Surrey. Bridget, Carol,
Gemma and me.

can work if you have individual characters in your display. However, where riders and horses are all in the same costume, having the same style of bridle for each works best aesthetically.

Vibrant colours work best in costumes, so they stand out in a large arena (see also Chapter 10). Imagine you get to the final at a major venue and you want the spectators in the back row to be able to make out who you are supposed to be. The costumes should be well made, and riders will need to wear make-up, otherwise they can look pale and washed out. Mind you, they may feel like this because of nerves, but it amazing what a bit of stage make-up can do!

Entrance and exit music is allowed, up to 60 seconds in length for each, and the time allowed for the performance is 5 minutes.

The Team

A team of four riders and horses needs to be selected, plus a couple of reserves. They should all be competent and able to work as a group. The best way of preparing is to practice so that every horse and rider can go first, last or in the middle to cover all eventualities in case things do not go according to plan! Some horses object to working side by side, so care must be taken in introducing them to this type of work. The most important aspect is to be able to keep a sense of humour throughout all the hard work and rehearsals – morale must remain high in order for the performance to come across well. Four riders scowling at each other by the time the big day comes does not bode well for a good performance! (A way round this would be to pick a 'monster' or pirate theme with 'baddies' in it!)

It helps if one member is in charge of costume, one acts as choreographer, one as practice liaison, and so on. You also need as many helpers as you can muster for the actual day, to assist with plaiting horses, wardrobe, tea and bacon-sandwich making and so on. You need a 'chef d'equipe', who should be good at making lists of necessary items and jobs that need to be done, as well as getting people to carry them out!

The day out should be fun, and it is a great way to involve non-riding members of the club.

Before the Quadrille takes place the costumes are inspected at close quarters by the judges, so it is quite important to get things right. This is the most nerve-racking part; it is like a Condition and Turnout class plus costumes. The inspection can take a long time, depending on how many teams there are, so it is important to remain calm, and to have costumes that are comfortable for the horses as well as the riders. Have an assistant or two on hand in case anything comes unglued, or horses become restless while you are waiting. If the weather is inclement, a supply of plastic bags is useful. Carrier bags make useful cover-ups for feet and headwear until you are safely mounted. Usually the warm-up arena and main arena are under cover, but take sufficient rugs, etc. to cover the horses until they are in the dry.

Do's and Don'ts

DO'S

- Watch films of the characters you are playing to help you 'get into character'.
- Choose characters and music that the audience will recognize, from shows or films such as *The Wizard of Oz*, *Grease*, *Cats*, *Pirates of the Caribbean* and *Braveheart*, or have a theme such as 'The Four Musketeers', 'The Aztec Gods', 'The Wild West', 'Cherokee Indians', 'Ballroom Dancers'.
- Take time putting together suitable music.
- Use simple school figures in an imaginative way rather than doing anything too complicated that is hard to remember.

- Practise with props and make sure you are comfortable with them.
- Rehearse with your understudies and make sure any rider can go in any position in the team.
- Make sure costumes are securely fastened and are not likely to come adrift when you are riding.
- Have a couple of dress rehearsals so you can get used to riding in your costumes, and to familiarize the horses with them. If a horse has a serious objection to a particular costume, either consider revising it or practise with the offending item until the horse gets used to it. (I had to take my 'Mary Poppins' umbrella to every training session – it was not only my horse who had to get used to it, but the other team members' horses as well.)
- Accustom the horses to applause and cheering. The last thing you want is the team to be scattered across the arena in front of the audience.
- Make sure your music is handed in to the organizers on time, and is clearly labelled with your team name, and where you will be starting from in the arena. Take at least one spare copy of the music just in case it does not play properly.

DON'TS
- Avoid making any last-minute changes of costume unless absolutely necessary.
- Stress can kill any artistic element to your ride. On no account get wound up about anything. Everyone needs a good sense of humour.
- Do not forget that you are part of a team, and are there to help and support each other.
- Do not wear the horses out by practising over and over again. A rehearsal using clothes pegs on the kitchen table is just as valuable.
- Do not forget you horse's passport and vaccination record. These will be checked by inspectors before the horses are unloaded and allowed into the stable yard. It is for your own peace of mind that all the horses on site are vaccinated against 'flu.
- Do not forget show passes and tickets for your friends and supporters.
- Avoid using exercise bandages on the horses. They will be standing around a lot in the inspection, and can become very uncomfortable, especially if the bandages are too tight. Use decorated brushing boots instead.

- Do not leave anything until the last minute. It always takes a lot longer to get ready than you think, so it is helpful to make a timetable for getting the horses ready, doing your make-up, dressing, and getting to the arena on time.

Tips from the Top

My friend Bridget Parry-James was a team member of Chipstead Riding Club when they won the Riding Club Quadrille of the Year at Olympia a few years ago. She is a grandmother and retired vet, and leads a very active life, competing in many Riding Club events. I asked Bridget how she became interested in Quadrille riding to music. She said: **'I like riding with others – four horses and riders working together looks very impressive and is very visual. As a child, drill rides were commonplace in riding schools, but as an adult it is difficult to find such tuition.**

I compete on King Rollo – a Connemara cross TB gelding I've done everything with – British Horse Society TREC, dressage, jumping, hunting and so on. Whether a horse is good at working to music depends very much on the riding, though some horses are more buzzy than others. When I compete as an individual, I think that finding a suitable rhythm is more important than the type of music. I also compete in Riding Club Rural Riders competitions which are not to music and you ride as a team of six in formation. It is a set test of Elementary level including, for example, extended canter, leg-yield and trot-halt transitions. I enjoy the sense of occasion, riding with others without music just as much as I do with music.

When riding as a team it is important to practise resolving mistakes that could happen, and to have a contingency plan. If one member goes wrong, it is up to another member to help out and take the lead, for example.

In practice, Rollo was kicked by another horse; consequently, in the next session, he absolutely refused to stand next in line to this horse, so we changed order. It is important for every member to ride in any position in the group of four, whether it means going at the front, the back or anywhere in between. We had to work on Rollo's confidence for quite a while before he would accept his assailant again.

My first experience with dressage to music was with Reigate Riding

Club, where we all had a hand in choosing the music. With Chipstead Riding Club, we had one talented rider who competed to music and won the London and South East Dressage to Music Championship, so she sorted out the music and the costumes. We all had a hand in the choreography and worked it out between us. We had a few lessons with a local riding instructor, Julie Winchester, who fine-tuned us leading up to the competition.

We found the music first, and then worked out the movements. It is great in Quadrille riding as you can use movements that are not conventional – the more imaginative you can be, the better! This is very different from normal dressage to music competitions, where you have to show specific movements in your routine.

When we came up with "Aztec Gods", we used South American tribal music, and included a lot of walk and leg-yield. The music was put together on a tape at home, and it was put on a CD by a friend.

It is important for the horses to listen to the music when you practise. People who ride with personal stereos are not letting their horses "in on it". It must be like half-hearing a conversation for the horse – quite frustrating I would imagine. Excluding your horse from the fun seems a bit mean.'

Chipstead Riding Club as 'Aztec Gods', leg-yielding on diagonal lines during their winning performance at Olympia.

I remember watching the performance at Olympia, and the most memorable part of the routine was where all four riders formed a diamond, and walked in leg-yield moving the 'diamond' around the arena. I asked Bridget what were her worst and best experiences when competing. She replied: **'The most difficult occasion was when an overload of competitive spirit caused a lot of tension in one team, which then became divided into two camps. We could only park one lorry by the arena, so some of us had to decamp to the car park up the road and catch the shuttle bus to Olympia, which didn't help.**

The best was winning with Chipstead Riding Club, where we all remained friends afterwards. We all ate together, slept in the same lorry, had stables side by side – all elements of basic team-building. We hired a big lorry especially so we were not split up.

There is a lot of tension behind the scenes at Olympia. Rollo had a box opposite the Household Cavalry, so he had them right in front of him – cannons and all! If you have a horse who gets a bit "hyper", you feel very responsible for keeping him under control – there are a lot of very expensive horses around and one would hate for anything to happen.'

Bridget's preparation tips are: **'Avoid "fiddly bits", as these always take longer than you think and you need several spare pairs of hands. I know of a couple of horses who were exhibiting signs of colic (Rollo was one of them) but the signs were simply of distress which was caused by standing around for too long in leg bandages which became too uncomfortable, causing the horses to fidget. Removal of the bandages brought swift relief from the "symptoms"!**

The best costumes we had were when we did *Thunderbirds*, as they were unfussy, and easy to put on and take off, which meant that the horses were not standing around for ages during the preparations.'

My next question was, 'Do you get nervous; if so, how do you cope with anxiety?' Bridget replied: **'I cope with pre-competition nerves by going into my shell, as I tend to become short and snappy, and I cannot focus on having a conversation with anyone! Rollo, on the other hand, stays very "cool" and actually goes better for having big lights and noise around him.**

After the Chipstead Riding Club team had won the Riding Club Quadrille of the Year competition in the morning, they had to perform a second time at Olympia in the afternoon programme. Bridget said they were on a great 'high' and were more relaxed than they had been in the morning and it was easier to show off and enjoy it!

On the two occasions I rode in a team with Bridget, we came third at Olympia with *Mary Poppins* but just missed qualifying as *Thunderbirds*. Bridget said, **'It is great to almost make it, and a great learning experience, which helped us enormously the next time. You have to work as a team and ride as a team – for each other and not as an individual, and this comes with experience.'**

9

QUADRILLE CHOREOGRAPHY

This differs a great deal from riding an individual show. When you are on your own, it is down to you to remember your test, and if you do go wrong, it is fairly easy to cover up your mistakes. However, when there are four riders, there is a greater risk of a glitch in the proceedings, but the trick is not to get too hung up about it. If one of you goes wrong, you have to be very brave and pretend your 'solo' bit was intended. (I speak from personal experience!) The other riders in your team then just have to pretend that what you are doing was intended, and carry on smiling, or they have to rescue the situation by some quick thinking. If you build in a couple of safety tactics when you are practising, you should be able to carry on and pick up where you should be for the next piece of music.

Movements need to look good when performed with four (or more) horses. Anything too complicated can look messy and can actually be dangerous, causing collisions. As mentioned earlier, the simplest of moves can look dramatic when performed by four or more horses, especially when well executed.

Pre-planning

Careful planning so that each horse and rider has room to perform each movement is important. Once the music has been selected, a rough plan of the routine needs to be drawn up on paper. The routine should tell a story, perhaps having four different characters (if using four riders); another way is to have all riders dressed the same. The routine needs to be practised thoroughly, and a good way to do this is around the kitchen table, which is marked out as the dressage arena, with four clothes pegs as the 'riders' (This is usually hilarious as arms get entwined during the manoeuvres!) This ensures that the riders know where they are going and that the horses do not become too fed up through too many mounted repetitions.

The experience of my own Quadrille teams is that, after many practices, we put together patterns using simple school figures in an imaginative way, making sure we had plenty of changes of gait and direction. At first, our horses complained a bit about working close together, and we resembled four dodgems, the amount of times we collided. However, after a few rehearsals, we could ride presentable turns across the school, and stay reasonably spaced during the manoeuvres. The horses began to become friends, apart from the odd hiccup, and we worked round any problems by adapting the routine here and there. All the horses became less spooky as they learnt to work together.

A couple of points to bear in mind when planning routines are:
- The three judges sit halfway down the long side at E, so the routine must start and finish at X facing the long side. (Since there are four riders, they start lined up with X at the mid-point of their line.)
- When choosing music, the copyright rules must be adhered to. When you send your entry in for a competition, you have to list each track you have used so it can be checked and cleared for use (see Music Licensing in Chapter 4).

Sample Routines

The following examples are routines we have used in the past for various displays and competitions.

MARY POPPINS
Theme
The movements we came up with tied in with scenes from the film, rather like acting on horseback, so there was a definite story to the whole routine. Of course, we had to watch the film a few times to get into the mood, and

we ended up humming the songs every day! The scenes we depicted were the 'tidying up' scene to 'Spoonful of Sugar' where everything was flying around the room before putting itself away, the part of the film where the four characters 'whoosh' through into the park scene ('Jolly Holiday') and the fairground scene where everyone is having a jolly good time ('Supercalifrag...'). The other part of the film was the rooftop scene, with the sweeps dancing around the chimney pots. The idea was to get the audience on our side by using familiar songs that hopefully everyone would be tapping their feet to!

Music

I found a CD of the film sound track, and listened to it several times, and made a shortlist of possible tracks. I then rode to these myself, to assess which suited walk, trot and canter, and also which had the most 'audience appeal'. Familiar tunes always lift a performance and you can feel the audience warming to the performers. I then made up a trial recording of the music for the team as a whole to try, and to work out in which order to place the tracks.

Choreography

Choreographing the Quadrille was a joint 'trial and error' exercise. I had a few initial ideas, some of which worked, and others which did not. Once we had the music at its final length, we tried linking different patterns together to see which were most effective.

Routine

Here is the routine, which is actually Reigate Riding Club's bid for the Olympia final, where we achieved a creditable third place a few years ago. There were no letters in the arena, or arena boards – just strategically placed trees in pots – but I have used letters when describing the movements to make things clearer. The words in bold print are key words in the songs so we knew exactly where we should be at the time.

Entry music – 45 seconds – **'Feed the Birds'**.
1. Enter the arena and halt facing the judges halfway down the long side at E.
    Music changes to **'Spoonful of Sugar'**.
    There is a small manoeuvre next (not shown on the diagram as it

looked too confusing!) where the middle two riders, 'Jane' and 'Michael' circle around 'Bert' and 'Mary', clapping hands together on **'snap'** returning to the line of four ready for the move-off. Move off in pairs right and left.

2. Ride large figure of eight in pairs, in canter, overlapping at X. (to simulate the toys, etc. flying around the room when Mary Poppins is tidying up). At **'whooshing'** music, converge at X in a line of four ready for change of music to **'Jolly Holiday'** into the funfair scene.

3. Track left two by two around the arena in trot (strolling through the park).

4. Cross the arena twice in a line of four, turning together each time (like merry-go-round horses on a carousel). The second one should be in time with **'Big Brass Band'**.

5. Another 'stroll around the park' two by two, finishing in single file at X.

6. Music change to **'Chim Chiminee'**. All ride a 10 m circle left around X in single file (simulating a chimney pot) – horses must be equally spaced. After eight beats of music, all circle outwards (to the right) individually for a count of eight (each 10 m circle must be eight strides) and return to the middle circle (to the left). This makes a 'flower' pattern around imaginary chimney pots (the chimney sweeps scene in the film).

7. Lead off the pattern in single file on the left rein, and turn up the centre line in single file.

8. Music change to **'Supercalifrag…'**. The routine 'hots up' at this point to fit to the excitement of the music!
   Alternate riders leg-yield in the same direction to the track on the long sides. Continue down the long sides, with each pair of riders one behind the other. At the track, make a transition to canter. Turn up the centre line at A two by two.

9. As the first two riders reach L (between V and P), all four riders ride an individual 10 m circle away from their partner, meeting as a pair again afterwards. Repeat further up the centre line at I (between S and R). Turn right at C in single file.

10. Ride a 20 m circle (in canter) in single file. (This circle can be adjusted in size/speed to fit to the music, so that the final halt is on the final beat of the music). Lead off down the long side, and turn as a line of four towards the judges, finishing on the centre line at X.

The Quadrille performed to the *Mary Poppins* theme.

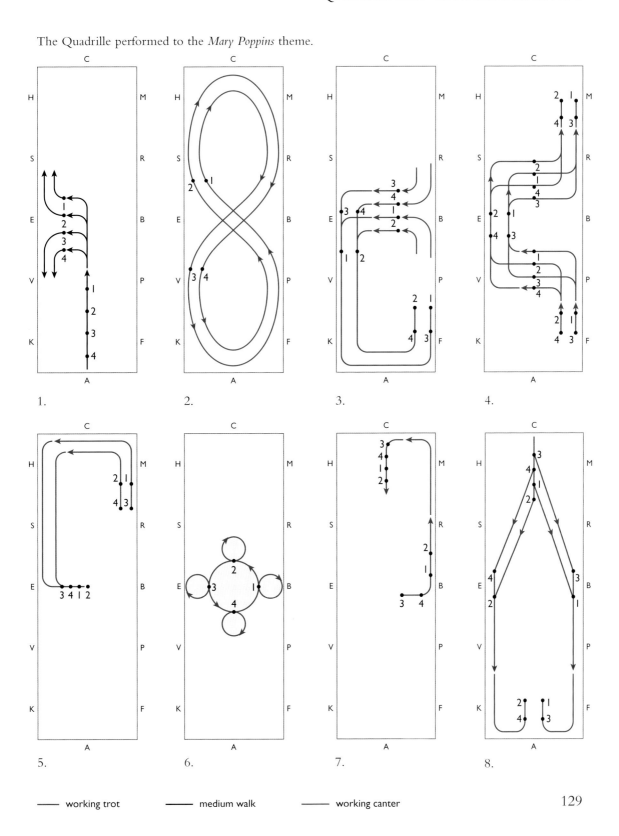

1.   2.   3.   4.

5.   6.   7.   8.

—— working trot   —— medium walk   —— working canter

Continued.

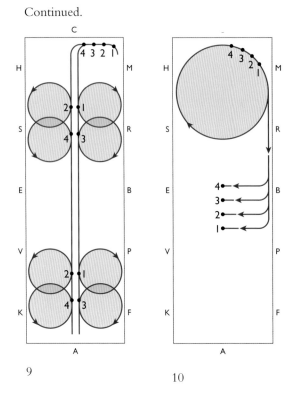

9   10

Exit music – 45 seconds – an instrumental medley of the 'Mary Poppins' tunes to get us out of the arena.

Costumes

The costumes we decided on were based on the four main characters – Mary Poppins (me), Bert the sweep (Bridget), the little girl, Jane (Carol) and Michael, her brother (Samantha). The characters have to be recognizable, so it was important to select key props, and items of dress which made each character easy to recognize.

MARY POPPINS

Of course, the umbrella was very important, as was the type of hat. A fitted jacket and skirt was her uniform, but I settled for a pair of culottes, which looked like a skirt, but were much easier to rider in. Amadeus was decked out in pink flowers and ribbons, which he was very happy to pose in. We thought this represented the floral aspects of the park and funfair scene.

B<small>ERT</small> (<small>THE SWEEP</small>)

Bridget did a great job with her costume, even down to the soot! She strapped a sweep's brush to her back, wore a cloth cap, trousers, hobnail boots, and a shirt that matched her horse Rollo's plaits and flowers. (His flowers were red, which stood out well against his bay coat). Rollo even wore blinkers and harness, which distinguished him as a working horse.

J<small>ANE AND</small> M<small>ICHAEL</small> (<small>THE TWO CHILDREN</small>)

Jane and Michael (Carol and Sam) were dressed as the two children. Carol wore a pretty yellow dress and straw hat, and Sam wore a striped jacket, shorts and boy's cap. Their two horses were decked out as merry-go-round horses in red and gold – as much as we could fit on them!

(For further details on making these and other costumes, see Personal Experience with Costumes in Chapter 10.)

THUNDERBIRDS

This is the routine we rode at Addington in the qualifying round for Olympia. Unfortunately, we did not get through this time as our music had a glitch and did not play properly, but the horses were well behaved, and we were pleased with the end result and the positive reactions of both the audience and the judges.

Theme

I really enjoyed watching old *Thunderbirds* videos for the ideas for this Quadrille! Bridget and I looked closely at the characters and their costumes to see what would look good. We decided on two 'Thunderbirds', Lady Penelope, and Parker, the chauffer. The theme was to go for a drive in the countryside, then launch into 'Thunderbirds' type manoeuvres to simulate the aircraft on a mission, building up the excitement throughout the routine.

Music

I managed to track down a CD of TV themes from the 1960s, but it was quite difficult to piece a routine together, as some of the sound quality was poor – which, in the end, was our downfall. The music is played on public address systems, so what can sound great when practising, even outdoors in a school, may not sound as good when played at full volume in a large indoor arena.

We started with 'driving through the countryside music' as an introduction, halted and saluted to '54321 – Thunderbirds Are Go', then proceeded on our mission to the *Thunderbirds* theme tune. We then rode to the theme tune from *Captain Scarlet*, another TV show from the same era. The theme to *Mission Impossible* came next, and the final part of the routine was performed to the *Thunderbirds* theme tune once more, using the last couple of minutes of the track, as it had a good build-up to a crescendo to finish. Our exit music was also *Thunderbirds* music.

Choreography

1. Enter the arena to **'Penelope and Parker going for a drive'** music – 45 seconds. Line up at X and halt facing the judges at E with Penelope and Parker as the middle two, flanked by the two Thunderbirds.

2. **Thunderbirds** music. Off in pairs right and left in trot, and come down the centre line towards each other.

3. Peel away from each other towards the long sides, then return to the centre line, again meeting up with same partner.

4. Peel away from partner, across diagonals individually, crossing at X. (Our version of an aerobatic display.)

5. Meet up as pairs at A and C; form 10 m circle around X, all on the right rein.

6. Leg-yield out and in (think aircraft doors opening and closing!).

7. Returning to central 10 m circle on the right rein, ride individual circles outwards on the left rein (this is the same move as used in **Mary Poppins**, but it fitted in well with this routine also).

8. Music change to **Captain Scarlet** theme – in walk, half-pirouettes from the central circle, changing the rein. This is ridden twice.

9. Music change to theme from **Mission Impossible** – lead off in single file in canter from X up the long side and turn up the centre line at A.

10. Ride alternate individual 10 m circles, going the opposite way from the rider in front, starting and finishing on the centre line. At X peel away to the corners in twos, one behind the other, and pass left hand to left hand at C.

The Quadrille performed to the *Thunderbirds* theme.

1.

2.

3.

4.

5.

6.

7.

8.

——— working trot   - - - - - collected walk   ——— working canter

Continued.

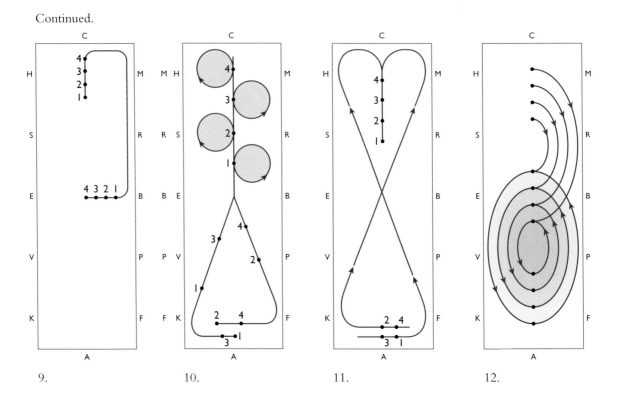

9.   10.   11.   12.

11. Ride across the diagonals in canter in twos, one behind the other. Finish on centre line one behind the other.

12. Music change to **_Thunderbirds_** theme – transition to trot. Start riding a large figure of eight, finishing at X on the centre line facing the judges.

Costumes

LADY PENELOPE (ME!)

The obvious choice was to wear pink. I did a survey of my friends and clients, asking what stuck in their minds with each character. Lady Penelope was definitely summed up as 'pink'. I had an old ballgown (bright pink) which was easy to adapt, and it was simple to find matching accessories in the local fancy dress shop – even a blonde wig! In hindsight, though, it would have been easier to ride in a trouser suit, which would have looked a bit more 'sleuth-like', seeing as how Lady Penelope helped solve the crimes in the films.

Me as 'Lady Penelope'.

Bridget as 'Thunderbird 1'.

PARKER (MATT)

Matt really looked the part in his chauffeur's outfit – it was the airline pilot's hat that did it, which added an air of grandeur to his costume of jacket, dark breeches and boots.

THUNDERBIRDS ONE AND TWO (BRIDGET AND RHONDA)

These two were dressed in blue boiler suits, rubber riding boots cut down and painted blue and yellow (by Bridget), and wore yellow sashes, complete with Thunderbirds 'ray guns' which were actually water pistols from Woolworths. A couple of matching blue catering hats were adorned with the appropriate badges to finish the look.

(For further details on making these and other costumes, see Personal Experience with Costumes in Chapter 10.)

THUNDERBIRDS MARK 2

This routine was designed to start and finish facing the audience situated at the 'C' end of the school, where a judge would be in a normal competition. We used it in a riding display at a local riding school, and it was performed beautifully by the staff.

1. **'Penelope and Parker music'** Enter arena in single file up the long side. Turn down the centre line as a four. Halt and salute at X **(5, 4, 3, 2, 1)**. Proceed as a four to C (the audience). Peel away in pairs in trot.

2. Across the diagonals in pairs, meeting at A and turning up the centre line first two followed by second two.

3. Proceed to X, and then peel away to the corners, ending up one behind the other.

4. Meet your partner at C and turn up the centre line in pairs. Peel away from each other at X and meet at A.

5. Centre line in single file. At C turn right.

6. Music change – *Captain Scarlet* theme – serpentine three loops as a ride (still in trot).

7. Music change – *Mission Impossible* theme. Walk transition at K. On the long side, turn across the school side by side. On the next long side, turn left, finishing one behind the other.

8. Music change – *Thunderbirds* theme – at H, trot in single file. At E canter a 20 m circle. On returning to E, trot. At A, turn down the centre line in single file.

9. Down the centre line in single file, at C turn right.

10. At B, canter a 20 m circle, trot transition on returning to B. Proceed up the long side in trot.

11. Turn up the centre line in single file. Leg-yield away to the long sides, riders 1 and 2 to the left, riders 3 and 4 to the right.

12. Repeat the leg-yields from C. Proceed up the long sides in twos (one behind the other). Meet as a ride at A, and ride four abreast up the centre line, halt and salute at X.

The Quadrille performed to the *Thunderbirds Mark 2* theme.

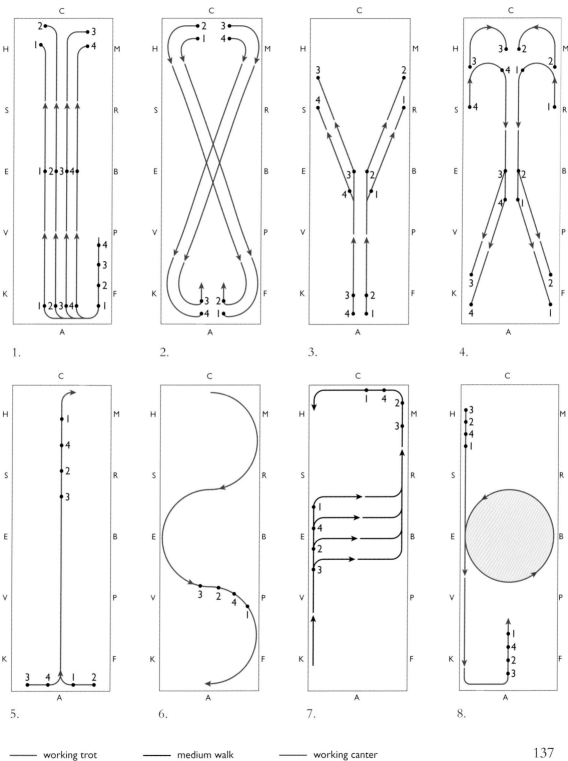

— working trot   — medium walk   — working canter

Continued.

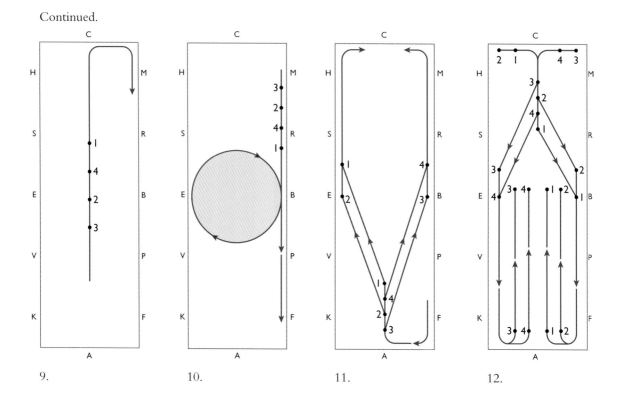

9.   10.   11.   12.

HOUSEHOLD CAVALRY

We rode this as a team of six for a riding school display when I was manager at Orchard Cottage Riding Stables in Surrey. The staff performed this routine at one of the many shows we held, riding six of the school horses – just to prove to the clients that the horses could turn across the school when asked, and did not always take a short cut to the rear of the ride as they often did in lessons when they could get away with misbehaving! This went down very well with the children in particular, as we all looked very different dressed up, and must have been quite convincing as 'real soldiers'. Margaret, the stable manager, dressed Bernard, one of the 'safe cobs' as a drum horse, complete with very convincing drums made from upturned feed bowls. She had her reins attached to the stirrups, as per the Household Cavalry, and her uniform was very authentic. Bernard was very well behaved, especially as he was the one who invented the 'short cut to the rear of the ride' trick!

This routine was used again at a local school fête with willing horse

The 'Household Cavalry' in action. We rode school movements that we taught every day in lessons. The clients were impressed with our ability to keep the horses 'one horse's length' apart.

owners from Allmanor Park Livery Stables, where I kept Amadeus at the time. We turned up at the fête to find the arena we were to perform in about half the size we were expecting! Fortunately, our music was a continuous medley of band-type music, so we could ad lib! Just as we entered the arena, passing under a huge banner, a gun went off to signal the start of the 'fun run'. We all managed to keep our cool, and all the horses were very well behaved, even Amadeus! The arena was surrounded by tables and chairs and everyone having a picnic. We were aware of people in close proximity, so were very careful not to get too close; hence our routine became even more compact! There was not really room to pass each other in two rides, so we all rode as one ride with me as leading file. We kept to a very slow trot, and managed to make an interesting little show! We were all very relieved when we reached the end without anyone crashing into the furniture! Luckily, we were finished and out of the ring before the 'fun runners' returned, though we could see them belting across the car park field while we were loading up the horses to go back to the yard.

Choreography
The choreography was quite simple, as follows.
1. Halt, salute at X standing side by side.
    Lead off in single file in trot.

The 'Household Cavalry' from Allmanor Park waiting to enter the arena at the local fête.

2. Turn down the centre line in single file.
3. Lead off left and right at C to form two rides of three.
   Turn across the school, passing left to left across the centre line.
   Proceed up the next long side towards A.
4. Pass left to left and change the rein across the diagonals.
5. Repeat change of rein.
   Meet at A in twos and come down the centre line.
6. Ride individual 10 m circles away from partner, middle riders positioned at X.
7. Proceed up the centre line to C, peel away in two rides of three.
   At E and B, commence 20 m circles, passing left to left. Whole ride canter.
8. After two times around, ride trot and proceed up the long sides.
   Meet at A and form single ride in original order.
9. C track right, and ride three-loop serpentine.
10. Halfway down the long side, turn right across the school side by side.
    Turn left at the track and proceed around the arena.
11. Repeat turn across the school left to right. Proceed up the long side.
12. On the short side, all turn down the school side by side, halting level with X.

The 'Household Cavalry' Quadrille.

1.

2.

3.

4.

5.

6.

7.

8.

———— working trot   ———— working canter

Continued.

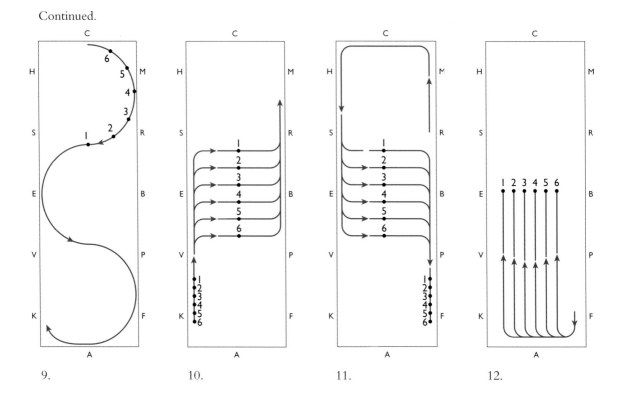

9.   10.   11.   12.

HALLOWEEN

This was a Preliminary test ridden mirror image by two rides. It was ridden by the same group of six riders as performed the Household Cavalry routine at one of my evening demonstrations. As it was Halloween, it seemed fitting to do this dressed at witches! A visit to the local fancy dress shop produced a selection of witches' hats, complete with orange and green hair. Capes were made from black bin bags, and riders supplied their own ghoulish accoutrements such as severed hands, bats, vampire teeth, and scary make-up! By using a set Preliminary test, with two rides of three, one riding the test normally, and the other mirror image, it was easy for everyone to learn. The leader of each ride had the prestige of carrying a broomstick! Often these 'casual' routines go down very well with the audience, as there is no great outlay on costumes, the theme of the routine is easy to follow, and all participants appear to be having fun (though nerves do creep in!).

Routine
1.   Halt in a line at X. Proceed towards the short side and peel off in two rides of three.

2. At E and B both rides perform a 20 m circle, passing left hand to left hand.
3. Pass left hand to left hand at A.
4. Change the rein across the diagonal, passing between each other. Pass left hand to left hand at C.
5. Repeat the 20 m circle at E and B, passing left hand to left hand. Proceed up the long sides.
6. Pass left to left at A, and ride a shallow loop on the long sides.
7. Go large and canter at the corner after C. Ride a transition to trot on returning to the corner before C. Walk at C.
8. Change the rein across the diagonal in walk. At the corner before A, trot.

   At the corner after A, canter.
9. Go large.
10. At the corner before A, trot.

   When all the riders are on the short side, all turn side by side down the school and halt level with X.

The 'Halloween' Quadrille (no spectators were devoured by ghouls during the performance).

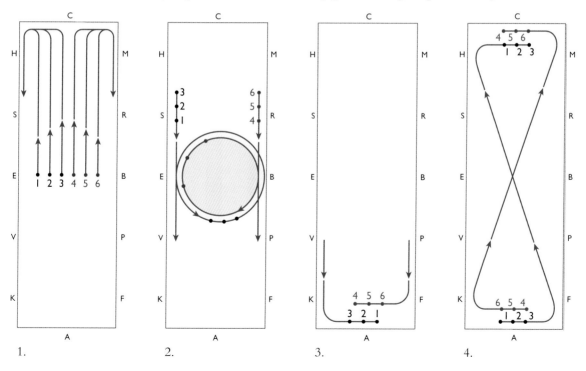

1.   2.   3.   4.

——— working trot   ——— medium walk   ——— working canter   143

Continued.

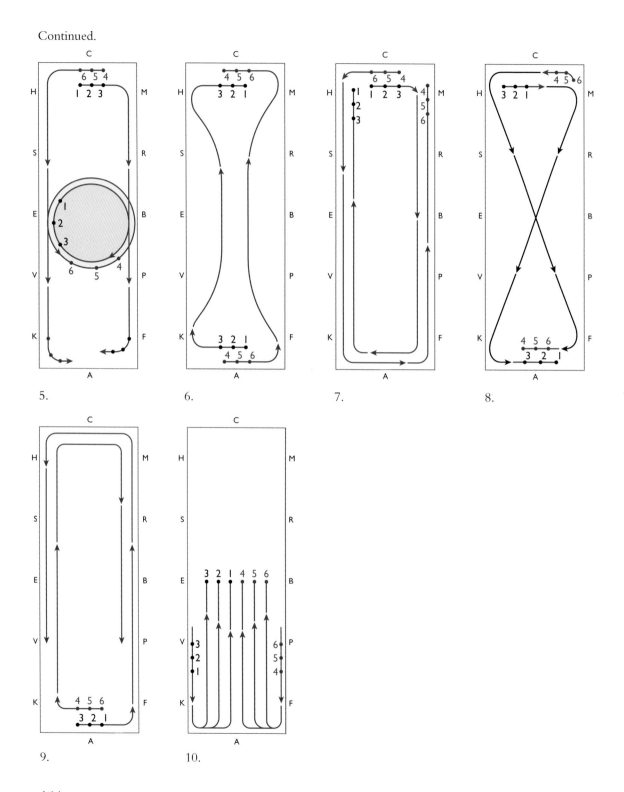

5.

6.

7.

8.

9.

10.

10

COSTUMES

Costumes do not have to be expensive, but you do need to allow a budget for each one. How much will depend in part on your inventiveness and practical skill, and in part on the seriousness and level of the display.

Fun and Ingenuity

If you watched *Blue Peter* as a child, (or do so even now) you will be familiar with the uses of toilet rolls, aluminium foil, fabric paint and sticky-backed plastic. A roll of duct or gaffer tape (which sticks anything to anything) should be in every Quadrille team's emergency kit! Make-up can add that theatrical look, so someone who is a dab hand with the mascara and face paint is worth their weight in gold. Second-hand clothes shops, charity shops and boot sales are all good sources of dressing-up items which can be glammed up, altered, painted and so on.

My earliest memory of dressing up on horseback was in the Pony Club. My friend Clare and I both rode a horse borrowed from Suzanne's Riding School, sitting one behind the other (we rode bareback) and dressed up as horseflies, wearing our school gym leotards and black tights. I made fly-like head-dresses, using two plastic tubs for each, painted black and held together with elastic. These, strapped to our heads as 'eyes', also had antennae attached, which were fashioned out of pipe cleaners with pom-poms on the ends. We won a prize awarded to us by boxer Henry Cooper.

Years later, I worked for some time as Chief Instructor at Orchard Cottage Riding School in Surrey, where we used to have great fun with

A convincing 'Mad Jock' outfit, hired from the local fancy dress shop at the last moment for the Scottish Quadrille.

our Riding to Music days. These went down well at Christmas time when everyone was in festive mood and wanting to let their hair down. We would give each session a theme and invite riders to dress up accordingly. We chose popular themes such as 'Western' (Cowboys and Indians), 'Scottish', 'Witches and Wizards', 'Animals', 'Black and White', and so on. Some riders felt a bit self-conscious and would just wear a single accessory such as a tartan scarf, or perhaps a cowboy hat, but others really went to town. Often two friends would confer about what they were going to wear, and would do a very good job between them.

People with young children often had access to the 'dressing-up box' at home, and this caused much amusement amongst the younger clients. 'Mummy's wearing my fairy wings'; 'My dad's wearing my mum's make-up, so there!' and so on. The 'chaps' from the Wednesday evening lesson group dressed up as Scotsmen. Tartan car rugs were put to use, as was anything else tartan – even a tea cosy found a new career as a sporran!

The staff could not get away without taking part (actually, we were itching to join in.) Members of staff dressed up as cowboys, with white breeches and black boots, and rode a very eye-catching routine to Western theme tunes. Two of the men had the idea that they would like to gallop into the arena dressed as Indians as the staff finished their routine, with the plan of ambushing them, so I tacked on another bit of music the girls did not know about, and Margaret took part in the subterfuge by opening the doors at the appropriate moment for the grand entrance of the 'Cherokees'. They wore huge feather head-dresses bought from a toy shop, but enhanced with feathers from an old feather duster lurking in someone's garage. Riding two of the school's skewbald cobs, they whooped into the arena, taking the staff totally by surprise and causing mayhem. The audience thought it was hilarious, but I do not think the girls were that impressed!

On another occasion we decided on 'The Household Cavalry' and set to making the costumes. We covered our hats with silver foil, made 'plume holders' out of toilet rolls, and plumes from red crêpe paper suitably 'feathered' into narrow strips. The 'helmets' were held together with rather a lot of Sellotape. We wore black show jackets, with a belt around the waist, white breeches, and white gloves which we all either had or could borrow. We shined our boots to military standard under the supervision of Margaret the yard manager. We wore sashes cut from a white plastic tablecloth and we made 'glove extensions' from the same tablecloth, which were stapled around our wrists at the last minute to make rather fetching gauntlets. The epaulettes on our shoulders were made of card, with gold tinsel from the Christmas decorations box stapled onto it. These were held in place with safety pins (I had to buy a large box of safety pins to cope with the demand.)

Margaret made her own 'drummer' costume. She made drums out of two feed bowls and altered Bernard's bridle so that she had the reins attached to her stirrups and could bang her drums. She wore a gold jacket and her riding cap. Her drumsticks were very authentic, with padded ends, but I do not recall what she made them from. I have a feeling it had something to do with stuffing a pair of socks.

The staff of Orchard Cottage Riding Stables as the The 'Household Cavalry', complete with 'drum horse'.

POSHER OPTIONS

While hand-made costumes can be very eye-catching, and particularly suitable for comic effect, borrowed or hired costumes can look stunning. It can be an advantage to know someone in the theatrical business who could point you in the right direction; otherwise the internet is a good source of information. Local dramatic societies may have a costume you could hire, but they can get a bit sensitive if you say you are going to ride a horse in it! You may have to swear blind that your horse will not dribble down it, and that you are going nowhere near a car park covered in puddles or a muddy field. Well-made costumes using heavy material do hang well, and are less likely to blow about if it is windy.

Amadeus and me, with Gloria and Billy, performing to classical music together. Gloria had borrowed these stunning dresses from a theatrical company. Amadeus and Billy had never met before, but fortunately they seemed to like each other, which made the routine relatively easy to ride. The plaster on my forehead is covering a gash to my head sustained a few minutes before we had to go on, caused by Amadeus kicking at a fly while I was bandaging his legs – my head was in the way and caught the blow. I do look a bit dazed!

One of my earliest demonstrations was in the New Forest. Amadeus and I teamed up with Gloria, a friend and client of mine, and her horse Billy, to ride a Pas de Deux at the end of the afternoon. Gloria borrowed two beautiful gowns for us to wear, complete with head-dresses made of elaborate hair bands woven with ribbons and pearls.

Side-saddle costumes can look very impressive. Long, flowing dresses can be worn – which can cover a multitude of sins. I had not ridden side-saddle very often but was up for the challenge when asked to join an informal display. (One of the other riders, who instructs side-saddle, brought a couple of side-saddles to try out beforehand – one of which fitted Amadeus well. If you wish to try side-saddle riding, consult a reputable saddle fitter who has experience with this pattern of saddle, and a suitably qualified instructor.) The horses all worked well together, and my steering was not too bad considering I had no leg on the offside! The four riders (including me) wore elegant outfits of various colours, with voluminous skirts and fitted jackets. Mine was topped off with a jaunty hat with ostrich feathers in a fetching shade of green. It helps, when wearing long skirts side-saddle, to have a 'stirrup' of elastic sewn underneath so that you can put your right foot (the one that hooks over the leaping head which stops you falling off) through it to anchor the skirt in place. Weights around the hem also help the material to hang properly. You can buy these from haberdashery shops.

Getting dressed in front of the horses at least familiarized them with the costumes to some extent, but Amadeus took some persuading to stand next to the mounting block with me standing on it in costume. Once I was on board, he kept peering at me out of one eye. He must have been wondering what all this stuff was, draped over him. We made our way to the school ready for our performance. We had worked out our partners earlier on in day at the rehearsal, but Amadeus took exception to his partner's rider in costume, and a distinct dislike to her orange skirt! No

Above left: Amadeus and myself in a borrowed outfit, ready for our first side-saddle event. He snorted a bit when I approached him in the stable dressed like this, and the mounting process was very interesting!

Above right: One of the other riders in a stunning orange dress. Having not had a dress rehearsal, Amadeus had a fit when he saw this rider and her horse approaching him in the arena.

amount of persuasion would get him to go alongside, so we had to do a bit of 'ad-libbing', which culminated in it all getting too much for Amadeus, who leapt in the air in a very passable capriole. I had to close my right knee very tightly around the aptly named 'leaping head' on the pommel of the saddle. I did manage to stay on though, much to my surprise. A dress rehearsal is never a bad idea!

Personal Experience with Costumes

My first experience as one of a Quadrille team was at Merrist Wood College in Surrey. Our theme was *Mary Poppins* and, as that character, while I decided that it would be easier to ride astride, I thought a large skirt might be a hindrance to keeping Amadeus under control, so I opted to make myself some culottes, which looked like a skirt when I was on board. I made an elastic 'stirrup' for each foot, which hooked under my boot, and was covered by material and thus out of sight. I had a drawstring waist which meant that the culottes were quick and easy to put on over a pair of dark breeches and my riding boots, so I felt comfortable when riding and was not distracted by anything flapping around. I wore a black corduroy jacket that I happened to have lurking in the back of the wardrobe, and found a hat complete with plastic cherries in an Oxfam shop. I bought a cheap child's umbrella from Woolworths. Amadeus wore white plastic flowers in his mane: I found these in the local Emporium – a great shop for unusual items and fake flowers. An Oxfam frilly blouse with a brooch at the neck finished off the outfit.

I liked the umbrella, as it was easy to put up and take down as required. I rode with my reins in one hand, which was a bit risky at times, but it did look rather effective riding with the umbrella up and it added an element of difficulty to the routine (which, if no disasters happened, could add to the artistic marks). We all had to practise with this, so that the other horses, as well as Amadeus, could get used to this pink thing waving about above my head.

Bridget, as Bert the sweep, found Rollo a second-hand driving harness and a pair of blinkers, which she also practised in. She even hacked out with him wearing the blinkers and said they were wonderful for preventing him from shying at the traffic! In fact, he never showed any sign of a problem with them. Looking back, it should have

Merrist Wood Quadrille competition. This our first attempt at making costumes and dressing up the horses.

Top left: Gemma as 'Michael', the little boy.

Top right: Carol as 'Jane', the little girl.

Bottom left: Bridget as 'Bert', the sweep.

Bottom right: Me as 'Mary Poppins'.

been Amadeus wearing the blinkers – he may have paid more attention!

Another prop Bridget practised with was her sweep's brush, which went through various forms of attachment to her back to prevent it bobbing around and catching her on the back of the neck. She experimented with various types of make-up, including boot polish, to get the desired 'sooty' effect required by a chimney sweep. She found a cloth cap, waistcoat and spotted neckerchief to complete the effect. Rollo wore red flowers in his mane to complement Bridget's neckerchief!

Gemma, as Michael, opted for shorts, which looked fine, but her legs did get pinched by the stirrup leathers when she rode, causing her a bit of discomfort. She also wore a striped jacket and straw boater (both from the Oxfam shop) and she wore a shirt and bow tie borrowed from her dad. A pair of white football socks and white shoes that she could ride in easily finished off the outfit.

Carol (who was the young girl, Jane) knew a seamstress, who made her a pretty party frock with a matching hat. She wore white tights and white tap-dancing shoes to complete the ensemble.

Gemma's and Carol's horses were sprayed with pink and blue paint (water-based) in various patterns. Unfortunately it rained, so the paint started to run before we went into the arena to perform, but the effect was achieved, as we won the competition!

After that, our costumes evolved further, in preparation for the qualifying competition for the Horse of the Year Show at Olympia. We were assisted in this by some other members of the Riding Club, who had experience of Olympia and were full of advice. Carol's costume was lovely anyway, so she did not need enhancing. Bridget's was also fine, so all she did was to add a few more flowers to Rollo's mane, a matching neckerchief to his tail and a bit more soot to her face! My umbrella was replaced, much to my dismay, by a lovely parasol, but it was rather heavy and not easy to put down in an emergency. A bit more lace was added to my culottes, and more flowers and cherries to my hat. Amadeus wore ribbons and flowers in his tail as well as his mane. The tail decorations had to be stitched in very firmly as he kept swishing his tail to try to dislodge them! He did get used to them eventually.

Gemma was replaced by Sam, who wore the same outfit as Gemma had done, but with tights underneath her shorts to prevent rubbing. She also wore a jacket with more pronounced stripes and her straw boater was replaced by a better model.

Sam and Carol's horses were decked out as fairground horses with red and gold saddle cloths, which I made from sponge covered in material, edged with gold piping made from water pipe insulation covered with gold material. The horses also wore neck and rein decorations courtesy of the local curtain shop. Their hooves were painted gold, and they wore gold-coloured boots. Amadeus and Rollo wore floral wreaths around their necks to match the ones in their manes, and had flowers attached to their leg bandages. It felt as though we had raided a flower shop!

We were asked to ride the routine again at a Gala Day at the Teachers of Tomorrow Trust in 2001, which we duly did. I went back to my old umbrella, but stuck some flowers on it to brighten it up. Bridget and I both rode one-handed in a double bridle as we began the routine, but opted to have both hands on the reins during the actual routine for extra control!

We then decided to have another go at the Addington qualifying competition with a totally different theme. Bridget and I bought *Thunderbirds* videos, and watched them closely to see if we could copy the costumes. I found paper overalls in a hardware shop that were the right shade of blue, and Bridget found catering 'hats' which were ideal for headwear. Rubber riding boots were cut down, painted blue, and had yellow

Waiting in the tunnel at Olympia. Our costumes looked rather glamorous and stood out well in the arena.

Me as Mary Poppins (again!) at The Teachers of Tomorrow Trust display a year after Olympia.

plastic tops fixed onto them. I made 'gun holsters' out of the same yellow plastic, and padded them with foam. The appropriate badges were made on the computer and stuck onto card. These were attached by good old safety pins! The guns were actually water pistols from a toy shop. The saddle cloths from *Mary Poppins* were covered in blue material to match the *Thunderbirds* theme of blue, yellow and gold. Bridget and Rhonda ('Thunderbirds One and Two') wore yellow gardening gloves to complete their outfits. Matt, as Parker, designed his own costume, which was brilliant. He wore grey breeches, and had acquired an airline pilot's hat and jacket (I hope the pilot knew about this!)

The hardest costume to design was mine, as Lady Penelope. In the end I opted for an old pink ballgown I had lying around (as you do!) and adapted it for rideability, such as securing the bodice and straps so they did not fall down! I tried to find a pink trouser suit, which I think would have been better, but time was against us, and I had to take the easiest option. I did complete my outfit with pink wig, tiara, feather boa, long black gloves and, on a whim, pink socks, which the judge noticed and remarked on. I do not know whether this was a positive reaction or not! 'Oh, pink socks, how cute' could be taken either way. (They do look under your clothing to see what you have on underneath, just to make sure that everything is neat and tidy, not just the parts that show!)

The horses all wore blue fly masks with a *Thunderbirds* motif, and blue and yellow ribbons in their manes. They wore gold sashes around their necks with a *Thunderbirds* badge on the front. We opted for brushing boots with a strip of holographic tape around them instead of bandages, having had problems with horses becoming restless wearing exercises bandages for hours on end. Boots are much quicker to put on and to take off.

Matt was the make-up artist as he has theatrical training. He did a brilliant job of making Bridget and Rhonda look like *Thunderbirds* puppets, complete with thick black eyebrows.

A great success story is that of Chipstead Riding Club, who won at Olympia as 'Aztec Gods.' They all wore identical costumes, which gave a unity to the performance. Their costumes were made by one of the team members. The very ornate gold head-dresses were home-made and the same gold design was also used on the bridles, manes and horse's legs. The riders wore flesh-coloured tights, and strapping on their legs to form sandals. They wore a dagger on one calf, and their faces were painted in a very dramatic pattern. Their cloaks were made from horticultural fleece, which was painted for the desired effect. The material shimmered under the lights at Olympia, and looked very expensive, although it was the cheapest option available for a large amount of fabric. The horses' tails were plaited and bound in keeping with the theme. They also wore Aztec-design sashes around their necks to complete these beautiful and very effective costumes.

Chipstead Riding Club Quadrille team dressed as 'Aztec Gods'. This winning Quadrille team wore identical costumes, which gives a unity to the performance.

Other Costume Successes

Here are some pointers based on successful costumes I have seen worn in action by other teams.

The *Wizard of Oz* team had fantastic costumes and a very convincing 'Lion' and 'Tin Man'. 'Dorothy' even had her little dog, 'Toto', secured to the back of her saddle. Their choice of music was superb, and I think that 'Yellow Brick Road' came into it somewhere.

The team who rode to *Grease* dressed two riders as rockers with teddy boy outfits, and the other two as 'jive girls' with full skirts and pigtails. The horses were dressed as cars, complete with headlamps on their chests and wheels on their legs. The latter looked to be cunningly disguised paper plates, but they were very effective and looked super from a distance.

The *Four Musketeers* matched identically, with identical horses, and rode a very slick swashbuckling routine totally in character with their outfits.

Two of the 'Ballroom Dancers' were dressed as Fred Astaire in very smart dinner suits, and the other two as Ginger Rogers, with lovely dresses which were well secured onto the saddle and the horses so they did not inadvertently flash any underwear.

Do-se-do-ing from the 'Barn Dancers'.

The 'Furious Angels' in full flight.

'Captain Hook' was aptly dressed, flanked by his pirates. The costumes were great – the striped shirts, headscarves and patches over one eye left you in no doubt who they were.

The 'Scarecrows' had very impressive pumpkin heads and straw that hung out of their sleeves without actually losing any (which was very clever), the odd crow sewn onto their saddle cloths and brightly coloured patches on their sackcloth clothes, and were accompanied by an Aunt Sally. They had music such as 'I've Got a Brand New Combine Harvester'.

'The Beatles' had the most super acid yellow and bright pink costumes and Beatle haircut wigs from *Sergeant Pepper's Lonely Hearts Club Band*. The music spoke for itself.

Other successful teams include a 'Cancan' team who looked very glamorous in their strapless frocks (I bet there was some concern about their clothing staying in place and the riders remaining 'decent') the 'Clockwork Clowns' who all wore matching sparkly clown costumes with large silver keys on their backs to be 'wound up' by, the 'Barn Dancers' and the 'Furious Angels' team, who had the most impressive costumes with huge purple wings. They must have had fun getting their horses used to them!

11

THE
PROFESSIONALS

*I*n 2006, I visited the World Equestrian Games in Aachen, where the highlight for me was the evening dressage to music, or Kür. The top fifteen riders from the Grand Prix Special the day before had qualified, and it was a spectacular event to a record audience of 45,000 in the main arena, plus another 5,000 watching on the big screens in Stadium 2. The atmosphere was absolutely electrifying as each competitor performed. The crowd was asked not to applaud before the final salute, but excitement overwhelmed the whole place as the grey mare Blue Hors Silver Moon came down the final centre line in passage. Sighs of anxiety could be heard as rhythmic hand-clapping started, which fortunately inspired Andreas Helgstrand to pull out all the stops for the last few steps into halt. The mare visibly sprang more and more off the ground, and halted to a great roar from the crowd, and a standing ovation. There was not a dry eye in the place and our hands were stinging from clapping so much! He ended up in a creditable second place. Isabell Werth put on a stunning performance with Satchmo to 'sixties music such as 'Puppet on a String' and tracks by The Beach Boys, and ended up taking third place. Anky van Grunsven pulled off a performance of pin-point accuracy to take a narrow lead (which she retained) with Keltic Salinero. Nadine Capellmann for Germany came in next. With her horse being named Elvis, her choice of music was obvious, and their performance was superbly choreographed to 'Blue Suede Shoes', 'Return to Sender' and other favourite tracks. She ended up in fourth place.

Left: Andreas Helgstrand of Denmark on Blue Hors Silver Moon.

Below: Action from the World Equestrian Games.

The buzz of the evening stayed with me for several days: the dressage was shown on prime-time TV in Germany so I watched the highlights when I arrived back at the hotel.

Having witnessed such a prestigious equestrian event, and realized just how daunting a big show like this can be, I asked some of the top riders in the world about their experiences, and for helpful tips.

Ingrid Klimke

Ingrid Klimke follows in the footsteps of her famous German father, Reiner Klimke as a leading trainer of horses. This Olympic participant is one of very few riders to have achieved success at the highest level in both dressage and eventing.

Ingrid began riding dressage to music because it is now a requirement at the top levels of dressage competition. She had a particular horse, Nector, with whom she was 7th in the World Cup Final in s'Hertogenbosch, who had a special passage music which he liked.

Ingrid says: **'I feel that horses have to get used to competing in a crowded atmosphere with loud music and not be frightened by the experience. From a judge's point of view there must be harmony – the whole thing should look like a dance. As a competitor, the best experience is when the music and movements fit perfectly and it feels like dancing. The worst is first, if the wrong music starts to play, and second, if the music stops in the middle of the Kür!'** Ingrid does not tend to become nervous herself when competing, but if the horse is anxious, she makes every effort to calm him down, and help him to gain confidence.

I asked her how she selects her music. She replied: **'For sure I choose something I like! I work out the choreography by collecting ideas, watching lots of competitions, and trying many varieties, and most importantly I look for the best movements and figures that show my horse off!'** Ingrid tends to work out the movements first, and then select the music, but she remains fairly flexible about changing both to achieve harmony in the final routine. She tends to use well-known tracks, but will have something composed if necessary. She says: **'I use the same music for several tests, but change the test as the horse develops. I teach the horse the routine so he is familiar with the music.'** I asked her if she left a margin for error: **'Yes! I do a second line for changes to repeat the one that had a mistake, and the same with pirouettes.'**

Behind the scenes at a competition, Ingrid sticks to her normal warm-up. In preparation she

Ingrid Klimke.

159

advises: **'Ride the routine at home often enough so that you know exactly where you have to be.'** The three words that came to her when I asked her what it was like to win a big class were: **'Thrilling! Proud! Fun! If I come second, I am pleased if I gave my best. If I am satisfied with my test, then it's fine!**

Richard Davison

Richard Davison has, for many years, been one of Britain's most successful dressage riders and has headed the national rankings on a number of occasions. He won a team silver medal at the European Championships in 1993 with Master JCB and was a member of the bronze medal-winning team a decade later on home turf, riding Ballaseyr Royale at the 2003 European Championships at Hickstead. In the same year Richard also became British National Dressage Champion and was awarded both the FEI (Fédération Equestre Internationale) Gold Badge of Honour and the British Equestrian Federation (BEF) Medal of Honour for recognition of activities connected with international endeavour. As a member of the British team, Richard has, at the time of writing, competed in three Olympics, two World Equestrian Games and four European Championships, and has been a World Cup finalist four times. He is deeply involved in the administration of the sport, and is also a television commentator.

Richard Davison in action.

The first time Richard rode in a World Cup Grand Prix Freestyle to Music (Kür) was at Goodwood in Sussex, which was one of the world's most prestigious outdoor dressage events. (Nowadays, all European World Cup shows are indoors). He borrowed some music and got the bug. I actually remember watching him ride – Goodwood was a great day out – and I found the whole thing totally inspiring.

Richard has competed on a lot of horses, and feels that you need a handy horse at Grand Prix level to make an interesting programme: **'You need to be able to string difficult things together with the horse and both of you must**

have the ability to remain relaxed. The best horses are expressive and rhythmical, which enables the rider to give a better interpretation of the music', he said.

I asked Richard how he selects his music and this is what he said:

'I have a cupboard full of CDs and I used to have an account with HMV! I would listen to track after track, driving in the car for instance, and I would think, "Yes, this will be great", only to find that it did not work at all well when I actually rode to it. With Hiscox Ascari, I used the same music for about ten years, but changed the programme as he became more experienced. As time went on I had percussion instruments superimposed and made other small changes in order to refine the programme. I started with a simple floor pattern and built on it – daring to take more risks as Askari became more confident and experienced in his work. As horses mature, their rhythm can become slower as they develop more cadence and strength, so you may have to slightly adjust the tempo of the music.

Speaking from my experience at Grand Prix level, a good test first has to have good technical quality and good interpretation of the music. It works best if there is a mix of emotions, with both crescendos and quiet phrases.'

Richard has had many memorable (good) rides, but he can certainly remember the worst – he was competing in Geneva in the late 1990s. His horses had shared the long journey in showjumper James Fisher's lorry, while Richard caught up with them by plane. After a good Grand Prix on the first day, qualifying for the Kür was not a problem, but finding his music was proving to be much more of a challenge. The night before the competition, he was looking for his music – turning everything upside down in the effort – and suddenly realized that he had left it in his own lorry back in England! He spent the evening going through the other riders' spare programmes, and eventually chose Anky van Grunsven's routine for Olympic Cocktail. Richard changed the programme slightly, which Anky later said she preferred! Richard confessed to not being the best at remembering things, and now packs his music in his top hat bag!

Coping with a big occasion and all the razzamatazz that goes with it can be problematical. Richard commented: **'Many riders forget how great the atmosphere can be at a final. People clap and cheer and can kick up quite a rumpus, so it is very important that the horse can** cope with this. Base your routine on what your horse is good at and finds easy. In my role as a commentator, I see many riders trying to do too difficult a programme in too difficult an environment. They do not take into account the effect the show atmosphere can have on a horse. Riding difficult things may work well at home when it is quiet, but it is a totally different thing when the horse has another frame of mind at a big competition. If you ride a test that is too difficult, you will lose more marks than if you play safe. It is far more important to build the horse's confidence using movements he enjoys. You lose far more marks by trying to be too clever and having a test that is too busy and hectic.

It is very important to have a sound check before the class. Stand in the middle of the arena – the speakers should be facing out towards the public. If the music is played too loud, or too quietly, it spoils it for the audience and the judges. If it is too loud, it can be upsetting for the horse. Music can sound very different in an empty arena as compared to when it is full of people.

You have to know the music yourself inside out. You need to know every single beat of the music, and where you should be at any given point. Different surfaces ride differently, so you have to take that into account.'

Richard has the radio on all the time at home as a matter of routine when schooling the horses, to help young horses become accustomed to the sound of loudspeakers. He says that, when being ridden to music, the horses do know where they are going, but he is not sure whether it is the horse who picks up the beat of the music, or the rider who picks up the rhythm and gives it to the horse.

On the subject of mistakes, and allowing a margin for error, Richard states: **'For example, if you feel the flying changes are not safe, then leave a spare diagonal in case you have to repeat them. If all is well, then maybe plan to ride say an extended canter. Having said that, it takes a lot of experience to know whether it is worth repeating movements, or not. You have to be fairly sure you can get it right, otherwise you are just compounding the mistake, and will probably lose more marks because of it.'**

Jennie Loriston-Clarke

Jennie is one the most influential figures in dressage, being at the forefront as a rider, trainer, judge and breeder. Riding Dutch Courage, she won individual bronze in the 1978 World Equestrian Games, and she has competed four times at the Olympics, coming 6th in 1980 with Dutch Gold, whom she trained from a three-year-old. She has run Catherston Stud since the late 1960s, is an FEI international judge and was chef d'equipe for the British Young Riders team for six years and is one of the trainers for the under-25s national training programme. A Fellow of the British Horse Society, she has been awarded the MBE and was presented with the first-ever Queen's Award for Outstanding Services to Equestrianism in 2006.

Jennie was originally inspired by a display to music at the Horse of the Year Show by Madame Hartel of Denmark, who won silver medals at the Olympics in 1952 and 1956. Madame Hartel was a polio victim and could not walk; she had to be lifted onto her horse, Jubilee who, Jennie recalled, had a hogged mane.

Among the many horses she rode to music, Dutch Gold was one whom Jennie regarded as very special. She feels that the horse's performance depends very much on the rider, but it helps if the horse is light-footed and agile, making him very manoeuvrable – Dutch Gold was one of these. As a judge, Jennie looks for harmony, fluency, and a good interesting programme performed well to the music.

Jennie Loriston-Clarke in action on Dutch Gold.

I asked Jennie how she selects her music – does she choose something she likes and ride to it, or does she do it another way? She replied: **'It is important to feel which music suits each horse. The only way is to ride to loads of music. Your choice depends on the type of horse and the way he goes in a rhythm. Ride to the music and play around with the phrases, loud and quiet bits etc., until you feel happy with your selection.'**

Regarding choreography, Jennie feels that it is the music that makes the movements. **'Use what the horse can do easily to show him off at his best. As the horse progresses in his training, more difficult movements can be incorporated. I use the same music for a whole season, or even longer. The routine has to develop over time as the horse becomes more experienced, but I do leave a margin for error. There are many more options to make an interesting routine with a well-trained horse.'**

When making a new routine from scratch, Jennie finds the music first, and then works out the movements. **'For example, I like a good waltz – people say the waltz does not fit canter, but I find it great for zigzags. Usually I ride to what I have available, but there was one occasion when a steel band composed some canter music for me. Andrew Lloyd Webber helped me once with a routine from a musical called *Jeeves*.**

In my day, there was not the technology there is now – these days people take a bit of this and that and put it together by computer, but I prefer to choose the music, and then fit the routine to it. I think this helps the performance, as you have to get a personal feel for the music with your horse. It is important for the horse to listen to the music when you practise.

My best experiences when competing were winning the Kür at the World Cup Qualifier in Berlin with Dutch Gold, beating Isabell Werth, and coming second in Paris. The Germans are a horse-friendly nation and sit quietly through the performance until you have finished, but the French were very excitable and clapped all the way through the tests, which made the horses very excited – it was difficult to keep all four feet on the ground at times! A circle of one-time changes brought the house down – Dutch Gold coped very well with the rumpus.'

At a show, Jennie advises: **'Go about things just as normal. I like to commune with my horse, and do all the preparation myself. I plait him and look after him. I think this is very important.'**

Arthur Kottas

Arthur Kottas has spent his whole life with horses. Accepted as a trainee rider in the Spanish Riding School, his talent was soon recognized and he rose rapidly under the tutelage of Colonel Podhajsky to become the youngest-ever First Chief Rider of the School. After taking early retirement from the Spanish Riding School, Arthur is now able to spend more time teaching and passing his great experience on to the next generation.

I asked Arthur what he liked about dressage to music. He replied: **'I love all music. If it is light and free it makes riding easier. It is good for the horse, and makes training more pleasant. Light music makes the body of the horse softer and more relaxed. All horses listen to music – the type of music affects them – some become calm, others more powerful, but some horses are better than others when it comes to competition.'**

Arthur chooses his music and the movements in many ways. He says: **'Sometimes it is best to do the choreography first; other times I just listen to lots of music. I experiment with riding walk, trot and canter, and then try to use parts of the music to fit movements to. The choreography is governed by what the horse is best at. The movements he finds easiest should be used the most.'**

Some riders have their music especially composed and others use well-known tracks. I asked Arthur which he preferred. He replied: **'I particularly like Mozart played in a modern way. But my daughter, Caroline, will never ride to classical music – she prefers something more powerful, so it depends on the age of the rider what type of music to use.**

I never work out my music alone; I have a professional do it for me. I send a video tape of the routine, and they compose the music with a synthesizer. I select which style

Arthur Kottas putting me through my paces.

Arthur Kottas in his role as Chief Rider of the Spanish Riding School.

165

of music, such as Michael Jackson. With a synthesizer, the rhythm of the music can be slowed down or speeded up to suit the horse exactly.'

Arthur tries to change the music for every competition, but says it can be expensive. He sometimes uses the same music at different competitions, but tries not to do it too often. **'I ride the Kür a lot – I also ride it indoors and out to get the correct speed. The timing must be good. You must know exactly where you should be at each beat of the music.'**

In each Kür there are set elements, so first Arthur plans the important lateral work, depending on the training level, and then selects the music. Then he works out the other movements that he will use. If he is judging, Arthur looks for the following in a good test:

1. Correctness of the movements.
2. How complicated the routine is, the right music and the timing of the transitions.
3. The music must be *ridden to*, and not just used as background music.

I asked Arthur what were his best and worst experiences when competing. He replied: **'The best experience is always when there is good harmony with the horse. If I feel this, winning is not a question. I have never had a bad experience, but I think it must be if the music stops or does not play. If I make a mistake, I must quickly forget it and concentrate on the next movement.'**

Behind the scenes at a show, Arthur feels that the training facilities and stabling must be as good as possible for the comfort of the horse, and that teamwork during the preparation for the competition is very important, so that the whole thing works together. He advises, **'Do not make any last-minute alterations in what you do. Once you discover what works, do not change it.'** He gets more nervous as a trainer than as a rider! I asked him what it felt like to win a big class. **'My satisfaction is whether it was a good ride, and not just to win a rosette. If I do not win, then I know I must train better next time!'**

For horses to cope with the atmosphere at big shows there must be trust. Arthur says, **'A horse is not a machine. The trust must be from the rider to the horse as well as from the horse to the rider.'**

CONCLUSION

To end on a personal note, I have had terrific fun riding to music over the years, and continue to do so with every horse I have. My favourite horse has to be Amadeus, who just enjoys himself so much every time I play music, especially so when there is an audience.

I hope that this book has inspired you to 'have a go', whether schooling on your own with music you enjoy, or competing either individually or with team mates. I have met many competitors in dressage to music events, from Novice level to Advanced, who certainly uphold the idea that it is not the winning that is important, but the taking part. Riding should be a pleasure, and I cannot think of a better way of achieving pleasure than riding your own horse to music.

APPENDIX

Equestrian Federations and
National Organizing Bodies

This Appendix gives contact details of the national federations/organizing bodies of some of the countries in which dressage to music is popular. Information about countries not included in this Appendix may be available from the FEI (see panel below).

FEI (INTERNATIONAL EQUESTRIAN FEDERATION)

ADDRESS
Avenue Mon-Repos 24, 1005 Lausanne, Switzerland

TELEPHONE
+41 21 310 47 47

FAX
+41 21 310 47 60

EMAIL
info@horsesport.org

OFFICIAL WEBSITE
www.horsesport.org

AUSTRALIA
EQUESTRIAN FEDERATION OF AUSTRALIA STATE BRANCHES:
NEW SOUTH WALES
PO Box 57, Glebe, NSW, 2037
Website: www.efansw.com.au
Telephone: (02) 9571 8777
Fax: (02) 9571 8044

VICTORIA
PO Box 616, Werribee, VIC, 3030
Website: www.efavic.com.au
Telephone: (03) 9974 0511
Fax: (03) 9974 0577

SOUTH AUSTRALIA
PO Box 1177, Marleston, SA, 5033
Website: www.efa-sa.org
Telephone: (08) 8234 2700
Fax: (08) 8234 2672

WESTERN AUSTRALIA
State Equestrian Centre, 303 Cathedral Ave., Brigadoon, WA, 6063
Website: www.efawa.com.au
Telephone: (08) 9296 1200
Fax: (08) 9296 1194

NORTHERN TERRITORY
PO Box 1244, Palmerston, NT, 0831
Website: www.4.tpgi.com.au/efant
Telephone: (08) 8988 1170
Fax: (08) 8999 6150

TASMANIA
PO Box 277, Brighton TAS, 7030
Website: www.tas.equestrian.org.au
Telephone: (03) 6268 5271
Fax: (03) 6239 6314

AUSTRIA
Bundesfachverband für Reiten und Fahren in Österreich
Geiselbergstrasse 26–32/Top 512
A – 1110 Wien
Email:office@fena.at
Website: www.fena.at
Telephone: +43-1-7499261
Fax: +43-1-7499261-91

CANADA

Dressage Canada
2685, Queensview Dr., Suite 100, Ottawa, Ontario, K2B 8K2
General Information: info@dressagecanada.org
Telephone: (613) 248-3433
Fax: (613) 248-3484
Toll Free: Toll Free: 1-866-282-8395

GERMANY

Deutsche Reiterliche Vereinigung e.V. including:
Bundesverband für Pferdesport und Pferdezucht (Governing body for Equestrian
Sport and Horse Breeding)
Fédération Equestre Nationale (FN) (German National Federation)
Freiherr-von-Langen-Straße 13, 48231 Warendorf
Telephone: 02581/6362-0

HOLLAND

Hippische sportbond, Stichting Nederlandse
Amsterdamsestraatweg 57, 3744 MA Baarn
Website: www.fbg.nl
Fax: 035-5411563

SWEDEN

Svenska Ridsportforbundet
Ridsportens Hus, Strömsholm, 734 94, STRÖMSHOLM
Website: www.ridsport.se
Email: kansliet@ridsport.se
Telephone: 0220-456 00

UK

British Dressage
National Agricultural Centre, Stoneleigh Park, Kenilworth, Warwickshire CV8 2RJ.
Website: www.britishdressage.co.uk
Telephone: 024 76 698830 (General Inquiries)
Fax: 024 76 690390

USA

United States Dressage Federation (USDF)
4051 Iron Works Parkway
Lexington, KY 40511
Website: www.usdf.org
Telephone: 859-971-2277
Fax: 859-971-7722

INDEX